Your Brilliant Inner Whisper

Discover why your Inner Voice is your greatest asset and how to tap its brilliance

Erec Lindberg

Your Brilliant Inner Whisper © 2021 by Erec Lindberg

Cover design by Ljiljana Smilevski

Published by Author Academy Elite
P. O. Box 43, Powell OH 43035
www.AuthorAcademyElite.com

All rights reserved. No part of this publication may be reproduced, stored in a retrieval system, or transmitted in any form or by any means—for example, electronic, photocopy, or recording—without the prior written permission of the publisher. The only exception is brief quotations in printed reviews.

Library of Congress Cataloging 2021907572
Softcover: 978-1-64746-771-5
Hardcover: 978-1-64746-772-2
eBook: 978-1-64746-773-9

Available in hardcover, softcover, e-book, and audiobook

Any internet addresses (websites, blogs, etc.) and telephone numbers printed in this book are offered as a resource. They are not intended in any way to be or imply an endorsement by Author Academy Elite, nor does Author Academy Elite vouch for the content of these sites and numbers for the life of this book.

Published in the United States of America

DEDICATION

To Dolores and Robert Lindberg
whose thoughts, words, and acts
prove beyond a shadow of a doubt
that unconditional love
is possible.

Contents

Preface – My Calling Arrives vii

Introduction – Our Journey Begins xv

Chapter 1   What Is Your Inner Voice? 1

Chapter 2   Where Is Your Inner Voice Located? 11

Chapter 3   What Does Your Inner Voice Feel
and Sound Like? 17

Chapter 4   The Truth of Your Inner Voice 22

Chapter 5   The Importance of Your Inner Voice 30

Chapter 6   The Freedom of Your Inner Voice 37

Chapter 7   The Power of Your Inner Voice 45

Chapter 8   The Strength of Your Inner Voice 53

Chapter 9   Becoming Aware of Your Inner Voice. 62

Chapter 10   Hearing Your Inner Voice 70

Chapter 11   Trusting your Inner Voice 77

Chapter 12   Acting on Your Inner Voice 84

Chapter 13   Living with and from Your
Inner Voice 92

Chapter 14   The Clarity of Your Inner Voice 102

Chapter 15   A Personal Journey with Your
Inner Voice 108

Chapter 16	Growing into the Energy of Your Inner Voice	115
Chapter 17	Your Inner Voice and the Fork in the Road	121
Chapter 18	Your Inner Voice and the Trailblazer in You	128
Chapter 19	Your Inner Voice and Your Highest Visions	135
Chapter 20	Raising Your Frequency through Your Inner Voice	143
Chapter 21	Your Inner Voice and Reading Higher-Frequency Material	152
Chapter 22	Your Inner Voice and Outer Appearances	161
Chapter 23	Your Inner Voice and Someone Else's Rules	169
Chapter 24	Your Inner Voice Is God within You	177
Chapter 25	Speaking from Your Inner Voice	182
Chapter 26	Your Inner Voice is Your Personal GPS	189
Chapter 27	Your Inner Voice and Living in Abundance	196

Afterword – Living in the Flow of Your Inner Voice 203

Tribute – In Memory of Jane Bishoff. 207

Acknowledgments 209

About The Author – Erec Lindberg. 211

Preface

My Calling Arrives

Never in my wildest dreams did I plan, prepare, or ever imagine I would become a writer, let alone a published author. As a kid, I hated having to write thank-you notes, so I couldn't conceive living each day, one sentence at a time, to write a book.

When I crossed into my fifties, my Inner Voice nudged me incessantly for over two years to take a writing course. I was living in New York City and the owner of a successful boutique catering business for the rich and famous.

Nora Ephron, the Academy Award-winning screenwriter of hits like "When Harry Met Sally" and "Sleepless in Seattle," approached me one day during a cocktail-party reading at Steve Martin's apartment for his latest play. Curious to know who I was, she asked for my card.

Nora became a catering client for twelve years…and generously catered to me by answering all my questions about writing.

I kept negating this inner nudge to take the writing course even though, on occasion, I would pick up a copy of "The Annex," an urban adult-learning center catalog with a selection of fiction and nonfiction writing classes.

I was being called to write about the Inner Voice because of my amazing successes from hearing and acting on it, which led to the life-altering experiences highlighted in this book.

Each chapter offers you a front-row seat to my adventures, with inspiration and steps to guide your success.

But what, exactly, is your Inner Whisper and how can you connect with it?

It's a voiceless voice…a feeling with words around it that pulls you into its power and wisdom. It comes as an energetic nudge or call to action.

Learning how to hear, trust, and act from this Inner Whisper opens the floodgates to manifestation. That's exactly what this book will help you discover, and it will forever change your life for the better!

In the personal story highlighted in each chapter, such as "Sandals and a Suit," you will learn how I used the Inner Whisper to tap my creative self-expression. And in others, like "Letter to the Landlord," you will see how I used my Inner Voice to pull off a total miracle.

At the end of each chapter, I show you how you can use your Inner Voice to pull off your own miracles too.

I realized, through all the ups and downs of my life, that a powerful force within always guided me and spoke to me. And it was always spot-on!

You too possess this inner guidance and compass to help you accept what you already know deep inside and to navigate your life.

But how many of us ignore that Inner Whisper or push it away, dismissing it as some silly notion?

I became aware that there was a connection between my call to write and this Inner Voice. And what better way to inspire others to heed their Inner Whisper than to celebrate its life-changing influence through my stories and experiences?

That was the aha moment that my calling as a writer had arrived! I could teach others how to listen and connect with their own Inner Voice by sharing my bold adventures, funny stories, and even my follies.

Thus, the concept for this book was born, and through my insightful experiences, you will learn how to connect with your Inner Voice and let it guide you.

Then, after the epiphany, came the tough part—the writing.

Finally, my Inner Voice won, and I signed up for a writing course at The Annex and what I presumed would be ten weeks of hell. When I walked into the first class, fifteen chairs were arranged in a horseshoe-shaped formation. I chose a seat at one of the ends.

It wasn't long before a glamorous blonde arrived in light blue jeans and a beautiful crisp white blouse with an expensive-looking, powder-blue pashmina scarf lightly draped over her shoulders. She floated in like a movie star and took the last seat directly across from me, at the other end of the horseshoe.

As the weeks passed, I would find out that, while half our class had already been published, the blonde woman was English and, like me, had no prior writing experience.

Unlike me, she lived mainly between London and New York, owned four homes with her husband, and led an international lifestyle.

By the end of the class, we became friends, and she frequently invited me to their country house an hour out of the city. Our friendship made all the teeth-gnashing over the weekly assignments worth the toil.

In the years following, we would share a spur-of-the-moment drink at a cool bar when we both happened to be in the same area of the city. It was also great fun for us to explore the latest new restaurant or attend art exhibits together.

Another benefit of writing-class-hell was that their beautiful pool house became my personal suite whenever I stayed over. I must confess there was nothing like hanging onto the "vanishing edge" infinity pool while looking out over the valley from their mountaintop country house.

I did not enjoy the weekly class assigned topics. Still, something started to awaken in me as I worked on them, arousing my interest to write stories connected to my Inner Voice experiences.

When the class ended, I hired my teacher to coach me in writing experiences from my life. I would fax material every few weeks, but believe me, I was not consistent or disciplined in doing my homework. She would make corrections, edits, and suggestions and then send them back, followed by a phone session to discuss the changes.

Though pulled to work with her, I felt some resistance in my commitment to grow as a writer. Truth be told, I'm glad I didn't have me as a student!

During this early writing process, I bought a Montana property created by a Western artist. He had purchased the 1912 train station from the local town and moved it three miles out to a hillside overlooking the Rocky Mountains. His painting studio sat, along with the horse stalls, in the rustic barn down the hill.

After I had completed renovating the station into my home, his painting studio became my pain-in-the-ass writing studio. I would walk down the hill around nine each morning and chain myself there until noon when I would head up for lunch. Then back I would go for an afternoon battle with my creative self, trying to birth what seemed like a book bumping inside my gut.

My writing sessions consisted of sitting in emotional pain, trying to write something of value when I had no clue about the writing process. Finally, I would become so overwhelmed and frustrated that I would walk over to a luxurious couch shipped in from New York and take a power nap to release feeling emotionally upended, fear-filled, and overcome with frustration.

The minute I opened my eyes following my siesta, I would force myself to get up, circle around the other side of the desk, and sit down. This created a beaten path in the carpet, with a full circle between the desk and the couch. I likened this back-and-forth between the desk and couch to a chicken on a rotisserie over a fire! I will also confess that something inside kept pulling me forward through this daunting and painful writing process.

I owned this property for nine years until the 2008 economic downturn deeply cut back on my catering business. I had to sell it for a song but was one of the lucky sellers who at least had found a buyer.

During the last two years in Montana, I quit writing altogether. With no place to run after it sold, my return to New York City brought me back to working on my book, which would evolve in two versions.

When I was nearing the first book's completion, a nonpracticing lawyer with no literary background expressed an interest in editing it. Since I didn't know better, I accepted his offer and never reviewed his work after the edits were finished. Facing a time crunch, I had him upload the manuscript directly to Amazon for publication.

While this first version was being printed, my friend Kathy guided me with creating a Kickstarter campaign to raise money to promote it across the country. I was very blessed to have the generous support of my family and friends who helped the Kickstarter reach its financial goal.

I believe that there are no problems, only opportunities, so when I saw the first book's numerous editing mistakes, I chose to move ahead without blaming. As you will see in the stories that follow, I trusted my Inner Voice to find my way forward.

The original book was posted on Amazon, but I had no clue how to market it, and I soon realized that offering classes and speaking engagements were not enough. So, as many authors often do, I hid for two years while I wrote a second book.

After that, I found myself with an unedited, rough draft of the second manuscript plus the original book on Amazon filled with editing mistakes. It was clear that hiding had not solved my initial dilemma.

After my trip across the country, I ended up in Medford, Oregon, twenty-five miles from the California border. I would later see why my higher assistance brought me here instead of reaching my intended California destination.

During my first few years in Oregon, I was referred to a prominent editor with over two dozen industry awards and twenty years of book editing under her red pen. Upon seeing the subject matter and stories in this book, she immediately accepted it, thus providing a stratospheric editing upgrade for the evolution of this book and its second birth.

For those who don't know, finding a great editor is no easy task. Due to such high demand and deadline schedules, they remain very selective in choosing a client. Yet again, I could feel my higher assistance at work.

With an editor who had spent her entire life heeding her Inner Voice and applying it in her work, this was proof of my ongoing higher assistance supporting the very message this book is built upon. In fact, after editing books in Sedona for over twelve years, she became known as the "Editorial Intuitive" because she listens to the Inner Whisper to perform her work.

This provided the perfect synchronistic energy to bring my book to its ultimate completion. I see it as a powerful combination of higher assistance and Inner-Voice direction. For me, there is a clear sense that, as a collaborative team, we are proof that inner guidance has been a pivotal factor in what we came here to do.

However, we both had some journeying ahead before the Editorial Intuitive could give my book a final coat of Inner-Whisper fairy dust.

Then came an opportunity to pitch the original book to another publisher who accepted me. I gained valuable insight into what additional material my book needed, so now I could transform it into my final vision.

I spent the Covid shutdown revising each chapter, designing a new cover, and changing the title to clarify my book's message before forwarding the new "second" draft to my Inner-Whisper editor for the ultimate polish.

And here it is. The simple act of reading this book will work to activate you on a deep cellular level to explore the last frontier of who you are and who you came here to be.

Now is the time to harness the power of your Inner Voice and manifest the life you desire.

Let's get started!

Erec Lindberg
Medford, Oregon

Introduction

Our Journey Begins

Welcome to the owner's manual for your Inner Voice!

Think of **Your Brilliant Inner Whisper** as a handbook designed to help you hear, trust, and act on guidance from the most valuable asset you own—your Inner Voice. As the last frontier of unexplored inner wealth, it holds the power to reveal the truth about who you are and what you came here to do.

This book recounts my personal journey over forty-two years of life-altering choices made by listening to, trusting, and acting on the wisdom of my Inner Voice. Consider me your coach as we embark on this magical adventure together.

You will note that each chapter throughout the book ends with a personal story from my life, followed by a section called "Your Inner Voice in Action." These examples are designed to help you see the theory in action and trigger Inner-Voice activations in your own life.

By sharing these stories and insights, I intend to trigger memories within you of those moments when your Inner Voice spoke to you—regardless of whether you heard it or acted upon it at the time—and bring those memories into your conscious awareness. You'll see how you've already had years of preparation to help you bring into your life the joy, abundance, and love that are the essence of who you are and what you came here to do.

So, before we dive in to reconnect with our Inner Voice, it's important to look at how we have neglected or ignored it, and the choices we can make to reclaim it.

Most of us were never taught about our "Inner Voice" at home or in school, even if we experienced brief glimpses of it as a gut feeling, hunch, insight, or intuition. We had no idea that we could rely on it to make daily choices and life-altering decisions with ease and confidence. We were unaware that it could lead us directly to our highest visions—those dreams and desires that best reflect our true self.

Instead, we have been left to fumble through life under the false pretenses of security, unconscious of the fact that we remain trapped above the neck in the chaos of our thinking mind as it plays "Connect the Dots" under the influences of the outer appearances.

Far too many people will never walk a path any different from the herd because fighting the outer appearances would become too uncomfortable to handle. They don't trust themselves with their unique personal expression. They don't want to embarrass themselves. They do not feel strong (or supported) enough to experience the "vast unknown" within them, especially when the process doesn't fit someone else's rules.

Some aren't brave enough to dig around enthusiastically in their passions if it means unemployment right after graduation or taking a "time-out" after they have been downsized. They fear walking the solitary path of "self-(re)discovery" if it means lacking a relationship or partner with whom they feel safe.

They have lost their personal sense of adventure, checked out, and are just going through the motions. They drop in front of the TV each night and go unconscious.

You Are NOT One of Them!

At this moment, you may feel overwhelmed, as if you're lost in the desert. You may feel hopeless or helpless because you can't see a light at the end of the tunnel. You may be experiencing a "dark night of the soul" when you no longer feel connected to your dreams or desires.

You are not alone in these moments of despair.

Countless men and women have passed through these dark moments and into the light of their truth. Thomas Edison spent a great deal of time in that dark place. So did Abraham Lincoln. John Grisham lived there for some time. J.K. Rowling gave birth to Harry Potter there.

Because they took one single step: they became still, turned silently to the depths of their being, and listened.

Like them, you can choose at this moment to hear, trust, and act on your Inner Voice's guidance and begin to walk your unique path toward who you are and what you came here to do. Choose to live in the vast unknown of yourself, just as they did in pursuit of their highest visions. Choose to stand firmly in a new you, despite all outer appearances.

You will not be alone! You will have your Inner Voice to lead you!

Once you connect with your Inner Voice, you will begin to see that it does not matter what you do for a living. Rather, it is about doing the inner expansion work while you are paying the bills and keeping food on the table.

You will soon understand that it is of no consequence if you are unemployed, lost in a sea of career choices, or feel unfulfilled in your relationship. Rather, it is about trusting yourself to pursue your highest visions simply by choosing to do so in each moment. It is about an inner knowing at the beginning of each day that the answers already lie inside of you.

Once you connect with your Inner Voice, you will begin to stand in your light—who you are and what you came here to do. It may take a leap of faith, as it did in my case, or perhaps a breakdown, for you to break through your thinking mind's rigid adherence to outer appearances.

Let's look at some examples as powerful reminders to support you on this journey.

Cracking open in their individually defining breakthrough moments, three internationally renowned authors have documented and shared their Inner-Voice journeys as they followed an inner pull to reveal their truest selves. Their revelations have encouraged millions of readers to activate and begin their journeys.

In her phenomenal bestseller *Eat, Pray, Love* (Viking Penguin, New York, 2006), Elizabeth Gilbert reveals that her life doesn't take off until she is lying prostrate on the bathroom floor connecting with the truest part of who she is. By outer appearances, she has a good life with a successful career, a loving husband, and a nice home—but until this moment, she has not yet heard her Inner Voice.

Similarly, in his *Friendship with God* series (The Berkley Publishing Group, a division of Penguin Putnam, Inc., New York, 1999), Neale Donald Walsch documents the struggles in his life, relationships, and careers until he hears his Inner Voice and begins to act on it.

Nearly a century ago, Napoleon Hill, though he had various short-lived career successes, could not make his life work until he lost everything materially. While on an afternoon walk at the lowest point in his life, he heard his Inner Voice for the first time. He returned home, inspired to review his years of interviews and research on a stalled project, and spent three months writing *Think and Grow Rich*, considered the best-selling self-help book of all time.

In *Your Brilliant Inner Whisper*, I share my breakthrough moment when I first consciously connected to my Inner Voice at age nineteen while walking to math class. This and each personal story I share with you is designed to activate you and awaken you to your Inner Voice.

I encourage you to enjoy the process of learning to hear, trust, and act on it as you become consciously aware of your own personal journey that has brought you to these pages. As with Elizabeth, Neale, and Napoleon, your Inner Voice will open you up to your life.

Your Inner Voice is REAL. It is triggering you as you read this. You might be aware of it now, or it might surface tomorrow or even six months from now. Do not worry if you can't feel or hear it today; it will come. Elizabeth, Neale, and Napoleon are three powerful reminders of this truth, and this book will inspire you along the way.

As you become more consciously aware, you will begin to hear your Inner Voice in different ways and feel its energy already residing inside of you. You will learn to trust it as you act on its direction. Those highest visions that you begin to achieve will further validate the authenticity of its truth.

Your thinking mind will, no doubt, create resistance in all forms, using outer appearances to discourage the journey out of your safety zone. But know that your "safety" zone is nothing more than a false reality. True security lies ONLY within you!

I chose *Your Brilliant Inner Whisper* as the title of this book because my Inner Voice directed me to do so, just as it guided each step on my path as I wrote these words. Every time I found myself above the neck and trapped in the chaos of my thinking mind's resistance, I would surrender, listen, and drop below the neck, choosing instead to hear, trust, and act on my Inner Voice's direction.

I never imagined that I could ever write persuasively enough to convey such a powerful message. But my Inner Voice led me through the vast unknown—past self-limiting thoughts and behavior created by my thinking mind—to write these pages for YOU.

Your Brilliant Inner Whisper is intended to help you break through the chaos of your thinking mind and to bring you further into alignment with who you are and what you came here to do.

Consider it the owner's manual not just for your Inner Voice but for your entire life – one of joy, fulfillment, and success.

Your Inner Voice will lead you on the truest path that you can walk in this state of being human. Join me in consciously choosing NOW, in this very moment, to begin to hear, trust, and act on its guidance!

Turn now to the first chapter and let my story activate the Inner Whisper in you!

Chapter 1

What Is Your Inner Voice?

Your Inner Voice is the most valuable asset you own. It speaks to you from your inner core located below the neck and above the waist. It is available to you 24/7 and 365 days a year.

It is your best friend. Your inner guide. A powerful mentor.

In his book *Friendship with God,* Neale Donald Walsch describes the Inner Voice as a "voiceless voice" or "a feeling with words around it." Let's take a look at that.

Think of all the times you had a hunch to act on something. An intuition bumping you. A gut-feeling that rang true. A sudden insight you felt urged to follow.

We use these terms to describe our Inner Voice as it speaks to us.

After years of honoring the process, I'm clear that the thought does not emanate from above the neck in my thinking mind. This "voiceless voice" is a feeling connected to a thought that rises from inside. The feeling and thought have an energy that we sense.

You may become aware of the feeling before you carry out the thought connected to it. Regardless, you will come to recognize this energy as it rises upward in you.

Sadly, most of us are not taught to recognize the Inner Voice in our youth or adulthood. While we may become familiar with the term, there is no focused effort to develop our Inner Voice. We merely use those terms to describe feelings or thoughts without conscious awareness of the powerful concept they represent. Since the concept isn't taught at home or in school, then it isn't honored as an important tool for both living and thriving in our physical world.

Most of us learn to ignore these hunches, insights, and gut feelings. Instead, we rely solely on what occurs above the neck in our thinking mind, remaining focused on and distracted by the drama and chaos of the outer appearances that surround us.

Thanks to the efforts of a growing number of enlightened individuals who have discovered who they are and what they came here to do by paying attention to their Inner Voice—and who have helped to raise our global human consciousness—more of us are becoming aware of the most important tool we have to guide us daily as we create the lives we want.

Only in the past century have quantum physics studies attempted to explore, understand, and illuminate this powerful concept of manifestation. Hearing, trusting, and acting from our Inner Voice's guidance is a key component in the manifestation process.

The voice inside speaks to you daily regardless of whether you are aware of it. Being unaware of your Inner Voice does not mean that you aren't honoring it. You may be heeding it and not even know it. It is important to note, however, that if you aren't consciously aware of it, then you aren't accessing and utilizing its full power as you consider and act on important decisions, especially those that can be life-altering.

Once you are consciously aware of your Inner Voice, trusting and acting on it from moment to moment, you will free yourself from the daily stress—even the paralyzing fear—that may otherwise hold you back from stepping into a more enriching life. Our Inner Voice feels (and is) directly connected to our dreams, visions, desires, and passions. These, in turn, reflect the truth of who we are and what we came here to do in this lifetime.

You may have a sense right now that it feels important to accept these concepts as truths. That's your Inner Voice being triggered. You can feel the energy of it. Take a moment to consider this.

Having grown to trust my Inner Voice implicitly over the years, I recognize that it has helped me to create and expand my life to its fullest potential in each moment. In fact, it led me to write this book to share my journey so it can benefit you and the lives of all who read it.

Let's start with a fun one....

My Personal Story: A Letter to the Landlord

On a bitter cold morning in February 1995, I stopped dead in my tracks halfway across my bedroom floor. A feeling followed by a thought had suddenly come up through me, causing me to react in total fear. I stood dumbstruck as I felt my Inner Voice push me to write a letter to my roommate's landlord requesting a two-bedroom apartment.

"What? Omigosh, the landlord doesn't even know I exist!"

My name wasn't on the lease, and I wasn't even sure if I could legally share a one-bedroom apartment in New York City with my roommate. My thinking mind yelled, "They'll throw you out when they find out you're living here!"

I felt overwhelmed. Why would my Inner Voice push me to do something with an unknown outcome like this?

I had been lucky to share the ridiculously low monthly expenses on this rent-controlled apartment for several months with a friend who occupied it only eight days a month when he drove into the city for TV work. In truth, the apartment was being loaned to him by his friend, "Texas Tom," who had long ago moved to—you guessed it—Texas.

I had never even met the man on the lease, and now my Inner Voice was pushing me to write to the landlord. I could jeopardize Tom's lease and the inexpensive living accommodations for my roommate, Steve, and myself.

I felt sick to my stomach. I didn't know if I could carry out what I knew inside that I needed to do. If only I could just skip over this day and pretend I didn't have this feeling coming up from that place inside me that I had grown to trust. Except, then, I would be living from above the neck in my head, which I had learned years earlier was NOT where truth lives.

I had trusted the voice that lives deep within my core below the neck and above the waist, for years, through all kinds of situations. It had always served me well, but I was momentarily filled with this thinking mind-induced fear.

I felt numb as I enclosed the letter with the monthly rent check and mailed it. All the while, my rational mind continued to scream, "Don't do it!" For days I lived in fear that I would find an eviction notice posted on the door or receive a call from the landlord telling me, "Get out!"

And yet... nothing happened. Each month I felt my Inner Voice urge me to include a personal note with the rent check, requesting the two-bedroom apartment for Tom (the phantom roommate on the lease who I had never met) and myself. I didn't dare tell either Tom or Steve about my letters to the landlord.

And then it happened. A man one floor above me, who had been living in a rent-controlled, two-bedroom apartment for over thirty years, suddenly died. Nobody had bothered to empty out the apartment, so now it had fallen in the city's jurisdiction. Tape crisscrossed the door until the matter could be addressed legally.

Months passed. Then one day the tape was removed, and workmen appeared inside. I peeked. It was small but had two bedrooms with lots of sun from a western exposure.

My rational mind immediately took control to push me to call the landlord, overpowering my Inner Voice telling me to wait, remain calm, and be patient. And then the landlord answered.

As I began to introduce myself and ask about the apartment, she immediately cut me off and snapped. "I've received all your letters, and I don't know what I am going to do with the apartment!"

I sheepishly apologized for sounding pushy and visibly shook as I put down the phone, thinking (above the neck—again!) that I had spoiled months of Inner Voice-directed groundwork with her.

Several days later the phone rang. I heard the landlord's voice ask if Tom and I were still interested in the new apartment. I said, "Yes! Yes, we are!"

She continued. "Someone will be right over to show it." When I told her that I had already seen it, she insisted. "I need YOU to look at it with MY representative—right now!"

As I listened to her cold and blustery words, my thinking mind raced. "You bet! Anything you say! What would you like me to wear? Can I bring coffee? Do you like warm chocolate-chip cookies, because I'll run get you some and send them back to you with your representative! Yes, ma'am! Yes, ma'am! Yes, ma'am!"

Yet, I heard a steady voice—my Inner Voice—say that, of course, I would be happy to meet her representative—immediately. Meanwhile, my thinking mind was in the throes of releasing months of pent-up emotions. When I hung up the phone, I did a jig (in place AND in quadruple time—not easy) yelling, "Yes! Yes! Yes!" I was dizzy with joy!

And just as quickly, I struck what I thought a military stance and salute would look like. While I'm sure it wasn't anything near a West Point standard, the action did serve to calm my emotions, and I returned back down below the neck. I didn't dare go back above the neck into my left brain with everything that was pending.

The landlord called later that day to ask about our decision. Oh shucks, I had not wanted to face the fact that Tom, and not I, was the current, fully vetted, and approved tenant—and the one who would need to sign the new lease. I stammered that Tom would not be back from Dallas until next week, but that I would Fed-Ex the lease for his signature.

She immediately replied, "I am NOT comfortable leasing the apartment to someone who hasn't SEEN it." My heart immediately dropped below sea level.

Then she continued. "Here's what we can do. We'll put the lease in your name, and Tom can be your roommate."

Never in my wildest dreams did I imagine that I would be the only one on the lease. Thank you, Inner Voice! I had just secured the golden ticket to the chocolate factory, with a rent-controlled, two-bedroom apartment on the Upper West Side in New York City, one block from The Park—as in Central. What a miracle!

If you haven't experienced the "pleasure" of the journey to find an apartment—a rent-controlled one, mind you—much less securing a lease in New York City, you may not truly comprehend how monumental this moment was.

I can recall my first spiritual teacher encouraging me years earlier to call forth the divine apartment, in divine scheduling, at the divine price. Well, it worked. My Inner Voice had consistently urged me forward as I acted on my divine intention at the beginning of every day through all these months—despite my rational brain questioning every move.

I would still not have this lease today if it hadn't been for my Inner Voice pushing me to move past mountainous fear and the outer appearances suggesting that I could never have what I wanted. Some years later, while I was traveling for extended periods, I found a roommate whose monthly rent share (which is ideal for him) covered all my monthly apartment expenses.

Oh, the joy of living rent-free in New York City—one block from Central Park! So much for the expression "Location! Location! Location!"—the new phrase to live by is "Inner Voice! Inner Voice! Inner Voice!"

◇◇

Manifesting what you want in your life is directly proportional to hearing, trusting, and acting on your Inner Voice guidance.

◇◇

Remarkable vision and genuine insights are always met with resistance.

Seth Godin

Your Inner Voice in Action

*Pulling yourself through the daunting
outer appearances*

When you start acting on your Inner Voice, your most significant barrier is facing the scary outer appearances.

Sending a letter to the landlord I had never met about a lease that my name wasn't even on triggered an insurmountable, outer-appearance fear barrier. It felt too overwhelming for my thinking mind to conceive, let alone act on. It was only by acting on the pull of my Inner Voice that I found the strength to carry myself past the fear to write the letter.

The energy pulling me to action represented a life-changing force activating me to accept my desire for a two-bedroom apartment.

Yes, I've had many years of experience acting on my Inner Voice, but it took every ounce of my inner trust to work from what I knew to be true inside.

No one escapes these overwhelming moments of outer-appearance fear barriers. The sad truth is that most people have no Inner Voice skill or preparation to face them.

There will come a time when you must decide to choose this powerful force for your life to move forward.

Trusting my Inner Voice that day allowed me to rent my second bedroom for over twenty years, bringing in hundreds of thousands of dollars—money I didn't have to earn.

Our Inner Voice is the most valuable asset we possess. The distinction here is that we must choose to acquire the daily skills of hearing, trusting, and acting on it, preparing us to receive the big blessings like the one in this case.

> Can you remember a mind-numbing experience when you were nudged to act on the Inner Whisper within but questioned it because of the overwhelming outer appearances?

Chapter 2

Where Is Your Inner Voice Located?

Your Inner Voice is located below the neck and above the waist.

As you visualize this area, you will recognize that it does not include your thinking mind. I'm pointing out an important line of division—the neck.

Notice that your heart sits below the neck. When you think too much, you are nowhere near your heart. The region above the neck remains too far from your truth.

Remember the real estate rule: "Location! Location! Location!" Well, this axiom also applies when you consider the Inner Voice and the heart—they both lie in that region below the neck and above the waist.

Hello, Lewis and Clark—where's your packhorse? Yes, you're going to be trailblazing as you explore the last frontier of you—your Inner Voice. Just take a step forward and remember to breathe. Here we go!

You are responsible for creating everything you experience in your life. *Everything*—no exceptions! This idea might be new to you and seem startling, overwhelming, and even unnerving. Just offer it up and put it in the shopping cart as you head to the checkout.

Let's up the ante by acknowledging that, up until now, you have created just about everything in your life through your thinking mind. You know… that area above the neck between your ears. Look at your life and ask yourself, "How's it workin'?"

This question poses a reality check, reminding us that we all have areas of our lives we would like to change—areas that we don't like (anymore) or that cause us to feel unhappy and dissatisfied. Why do we continue to tolerate these issues day after day, year in and year out? "How's it workin' for ya?" holds your thinking mind accountable for all its past choices and actions.

You will soon come to see that your Inner Voice is a powerful change agent. It can "un-create" anything that your thinking mind has conceived. It can save you from compromising situations, from "What was I thinking when I bought that shirt?" and "Why did I make that commitment to be in my cousin's wedding?" to "Where was my head when I started dating so-and-so?"

Yes, uncreate whatever you no longer want in your life. Through your Inner Voice, you will become aware of those things you never wanted in the first place. But your thinking mind didn't know it at the time or base its choices on outer appearances that do not reflect your truth. Transitioning below the neck and allowing your Inner Voice to guide you forces a powerful redirection of your life.

Because we were never taught about our Inner Voice, we have used, almost exclusively, our thinking mind (which, in turn, has relied on the outer appearances) to make our life decisions and choices. But our thinking mind doesn't realize that the outer appearances aren't real. Rather, they are just our thinking mind's version of reality based on its previous experiences and the belief systems it has created around them.

Your Brilliant Inner Whisper, along with your Inner Voice, will help you to become consciously aware of your real truth. And it has nothing to do with outer appearances. Allowing your Inner Voice to lead you forward will make for one heck of an interesting ride as you awaken to the new you. And along the way, you're going to have some fun too!

Two Bicycles

One June day I felt pulled to buy a mountain bike to ride around New York City. I was living on Manhattan's Upper West Side, a block from Central Park and four blocks from a path that runs along the Hudson River.

As I walked into my local bike shop, I discovered the most beautiful bike I had ever seen. I heard myself gushing to the salesperson about the bike's unique design and beauty, asking what it was called, as well as the price. It wasn't a mountain bike, but a road bike called a "Y Foil," made by Trek. And it had a price tag of four thousand dollars—and that was years ago!

Since my budget was less than half of that figure, I headed for the mountain bikes. I took several brands out for test rides, always feeling numb when I looked at the Y Foil each time I returned to the shop. My thinking mind rationalized that I could "deal" with a non-Y Foil bike, and I finally left with a (sort of) beautiful yellow "Specialized" brand mountain bike and hit the paths around the city.

Several days later while running errands, I saw a man on a cobalt blue Y Foil, my favorite bike color at the time. At that moment, my Inner Voice finally got the better of my thinking mind, wrapping it with duct tape as it pulled me back to the bike shop.

I asked about the Y Foil, and they said that it had just gone on sale for two thousand seven hundred dollars!

Immediately, my Inner Voice pushed me to order the Y Foil in cobalt blue. But it also told me to wait for a couple of months to pick it up on my birthday. I don't think I have ever experienced that level of anticipation over time. It was a shock to my system!

The day was sunny and beautiful when I picked up that bike. I experienced such an immense feeling of gratitude that welled up inside me when I put my foot on the pedal and rode my very own cobalt blue Y Foil down the street.

Acting from inside brought a deeper level of satisfaction and joy than I had ever experienced. I love my Inner Voice for guiding me forward, to claim what my thinking mind told me I didn't need or couldn't have.

I have never seen another cobalt blue Y Foil anywhere since I saw that one on the street, which activated me to return to the bike store to find that mine was on sale. Months later, while out riding, I suddenly remembered that a year earlier I had visited a friend at a sports networking event. As I was leaving, I walked by a cobalt blue Y Foil—perhaps it was the prior one I saw on the street.

There are moments when my Inner Voice has shown me ahead of time—if I am willing to accept it— some blessing that is coming into my life.

There is nothing so terrible as activity without insight.

Johann Wolfgang van Goethe

Your Inner Voice in Action

Activating divine scheduling and higher assistance when you need it

I did not act on the energetic attraction to the Y Foil with the four-thousand-dollar price tag because I did not care for the gold color and my rational mind was yelling, "It's too expensive!" It was the unique frame design that activated my Inner Voice.

My higher assistance and divine scheduling kicked in, placing me on the street in my neighborhood at just the right time to see a cobalt blue Y Foil. Your higher assistance and divine scheduling are active whenever you honor your Inner Voice.

Since I believe there is no coincidence, I knew my higher assistance had just given me another chance at the bike of my dreams, but now in my favorite bike color.

This sighting was enough to override my thinking mind's money resistance, so I immediately headed back to the bike shop to inquire about the blue Y Foil.

I walked away from this experience with the clarity that I must never settle for less when acting on my Inner Voice… and, above all, the importance of following my Inner Voice's pull to the very end.

> Can you recall a situation when divine scheduling put you in just the right place at the right time?
>
> Did you act on what you were being shown?

Chapter 3

What Does Your Inner Voice Feel and Sound Like?

Our Inner Voice attracts our attention in many ways. It often appears as:

- a warm, welcome feeling that comes over us,
- a chill that comes up through us,
- a tingle at the back of our neck in recognition of a truth coming to mind,
- a thought that sounds or feels true to us although we can't explain why,
- an Inner Voice "thought" that is "louder" than the "thoughts" of our rational mind,
- a spontaneous insight spoken directly from our lips in conversation,
- a feeling or thought from outside our thinking mind that simply appears in it,
- a gentle push that is just enough to motivate a simple action, like picking up the phone to call someone,
- a calmness that comes for several minutes, hours, or days before we become aware of what we will be shown, and
- a conversation between our Inner Voice and thinking mind. Back and forth. Back and forth. We feel that inner dialogue surface from within us.

My Inner Voice can be quite tenacious; at times, it will not leave me alone. It runs the same sentence, picture, feeling, or thought around in my consciousness until it triggers me to pay attention. Most often it must be that insistent to push my thinking mind beyond its comfort zone.

Such instances include opening to a change in circumstances or a new situation unexpectedly changing my schedule, accepting something that I know is true for me, accepting something that my thinking mind says I can't afford or have, or accepting that I have the wisdom to actually do or achieve my highest visions.

The force of my Inner Voice push is often directly proportional to the resistance of my thinking mind to release its perception of the outer appearances.

Shaving at the Sink

One day as I was shaving at my bathroom sink, the thought of a childhood neighbor from Montana whom I had neither seen nor spoken to in fifteen years came into my thinking mind. I knew there must be a reason for her to suddenly appear in my thoughts in the middle of shaving. So, I walked into my office, and, after five phone calls, tracked her down. She was now living in Iowa.

I told her about the inner push motivating me to call and asked if she was all right. She confessed that she faced difficult circumstances, having married a man a few months earlier and then moving to Iowa for his job. She said she was deeply unhappy and felt trapped there with her two children (from an earlier marriage) because she had leased out her house in Washington state.

Just as my Inner Voice pushed me to make that initial call, it then continued to push me to give her daily support over the phone during the coming weeks. I could hear the truth of my Inner Voice rise inside me during our phone calls. These conversations, in turn, activated her inner truth to start making the necessary changes in her life.

Within a month she had left her husband, packed up, and moved out of Iowa. Within three years, she was living her childhood dream, having sold her home in Washington to move back to the family farm in Montana, where she was earning a good living from her home office and enjoying her life.

Honoring the feeling of my truth that came up inside while I was shaving helped a childhood friend to get back on track with her life. My Inner Voice continued to push me to work with her by phone all through those years of transition.

Honoring our inner guidance is not just about obtaining all the toys we want; it's about helping the people in our lives. If we don't honor that feeling as it emerges, then we cannot serve those who are important to us. We are all here to help each other. I have written this book to remind you that you already know this deep inside yourself.

Your Inner Voice carries a message of truth for you and the people around you. Your Inner Voice knows no state lines, time zones, or distances. It may speak to you at any time. It can even be heard while you shave—if you are consciously aware and willing to listen.

Living from your inner voice, you are a beacon of light illuminating the truth in others, guiding them closer to who they are and what they came here to do.

Listen to your own voice, your own soul. Too many people listen to the noise of the world instead of themselves.

Leon Brown

Your Inner Voice in Action

*Making a difference by assisting
the people you care about*

When the nudge came to call my friend, I immediately experienced several seconds of thinking-mind resistance, not wanting to take any time out of my schedule.

Most of us do not follow through with acting on our Inner Voice regarding family, colleagues, or friends. Our thinking mind doesn't want to stick its neck out, be laughed at, look stupid, be judged, or be wrong.

It can become a life-changing gift when you use Inner-Voice direction to assist the people in your life. You will have a raised awareness for supporting loved ones, close friends, and even people you're involved in business or community dealings. Your inner guidance will also bring clarity for specific ways to approach each situation.

We must decide to no longer let our busy schedule become a roadblock to following through with what our Inner Whisper is pulling us to do for others.

By the time I had finished shaving, my resistance had lessened. Once again, I had remembered my commitment to live from the whisper inside, especially if it could make a difference for people I care about. Imagine the immense value this will have over the long haul.

> Who has your Inner Voice been nudging you to contact to offer your insightful assistance?

Chapter 4

The Truth of Your Inner Voice

We often forget what is true for us.

We cannot hear or feel what is true for us.

We do not honor what is true for us even when we are aware of it.

Conditioned to carry out our lives unconsciously, we go through the motions and function one-hundred percent from our thinking minds, completely unaware of our Inner Voice. Even if we are conscious, the stress of our hectic lifestyles prevents us from gaining a clear perspective on our truth. In most instances, we are definitely not present in the moment.

Those of us who are awake and aware may still refuse to face the fact that our belief systems don't seem to fit our lives. What we think we believe is more often NOT related to our truth.

For example, most states maintain a maximum speed limit of seventy-five miles per hour. Even the least expensive new car can hit that with ease. Yet we still see advertising for new high-performance cars with speedometers that go up to one hundred fifty miles per hour—double the legal speed limit.

Where are we going to use that horsepower without breaking the law? Why do we think we need this much engine power? Why do we work so hard to pay for these expensive, high-performance toys?

We have lost touch with what is true for us in all the commercial advertising noise—the "outer appearances."

I'm not saying that owning one of these automobiles is wrong. I have driven several of them, in fact! But in each case, I was directed by my Inner Voice to these vehicles through a divine turn of events. There was no question that they had my name on them and I was clear about the circumstances that fit their arrival into my life.

The distinction lies in that most of us are not hearing what is true for us. Instead, we focus on the outer appearances, with their bombardment of marketing, advertising, and peer pressure telling us what we need and who we are. And we hear these messages consistently throughout each day in all areas of our lives… because we remain stuck above the neck in our thinking mind.

Your thinking mind would never allow you to drive your mother's twenty-five-year-old car—you know, the one with the big dent in the center of the trunk from the time she backed into the UPS truck—to a restaurant with valet parking and with your friends in the backseat!

But once you transition below the neck, you might be told to surprise your friends and drive to that restaurant in the old rig. Your Inner Voice will know if it's for their egos' highest good. Try not to smile above the neck at that moment!

Look at how we pack our daily schedules at the risk of feeling stressed and overwhelmed. Or how we justify the expense of certain material purchases we think we need but then feel pain every month when the bill comes due. Or order extra courses at a restaurant when we aren't even hungry, but everyone else is ordering them so we feel obligated to do the same.

We overextend ourselves to meet the expectations of others based on these outer appearances. Many of us spend significant amounts of our hard-earned money on things that don't fit our life. We do not listen or hear the truth of our Inner Voice.

It is time to change.

Once you connect with your Inner Voice, you will live in a conscious awareness that will help you to create a lifestyle more aligned with your truth. For example, ask yourself:

How can I cut my expenses that no longer fit my life?

What can I sell that no longer serves me?

How have my social needs changed?

Do I truly enjoy doing what I'm pursuing in my free time?

Your world will greatly expand in ways you never saw coming when you drop below the neck and allow your Inner Voice to guide changes in your life that no longer fit who you truly are.

Home Office and "I Don't Do Food"

At the age of thirty-one, my Inner Voice directed me to move from Montana to New York City to pursue a career, singing jingles on radio and TV commercials. I had previously owned and managed a successful restaurant for six years, but my Inner Voice wouldn't let me sit back on my laurels. I was bored out of my skin.

New York City eats up money, and with the cost of singing coaches and classes, in addition to living expenses, I had to create some type of supplementary income. So, I started working as a waiter for catering companies. This provided a flexible schedule to pursue singing—and also a great opportunity to see some of the most incredible private living spaces in this city and meet their occupants. As time passed, many of these clients approached me directly to cater their parties.

Being consciously aware, I had to face what was true for me at that point in my life: having owned a restaurant, I knew that I never wanted to manage a commercial kitchen again.

You may wonder how I could operate a catering business without a kitchen. Well, I began by making all my decisions from below the neck. I started a catering business. And I didn't do food!

Acting from my Inner Voice guidance about my truth, I could stay below the neck, listen to my Inner Whisper, and take one step at a time.

You will be shown the same in your life choices. Your Inner Voice will lead you.

Another truth at that time was that I believed it a wonderful luxury and necessity to earn a living out of my home office. You know the drill… wear the pajamas while you're making money. Just because I grew up in Montana doesn't mean that I don't enjoy looking out at the snow from inside my warm and cozy office!

I succeeded in managing a thriving boutique catering business with the rich and famous of New York as my clients from that home office in my apartment. All I did was surrender to my truth, and then let my Inner Voice guide me along that path.

An additional truth is that I work only with clients who I absolutely enjoy. I will not work again with anyone who does not appreciate my staff and our efforts. It's one of the perks of being the boss.

My truth comes first. As will yours.

Had I let my thinking mind have any say about owning a catering business without a kitchen and based out of a home office, it would have said, "NO, you can't do that!" My Inner Voice, however, knew what was true for me. I just honored that inner truth every step of the way as my Inner Voice led me forward.

The truth of your Inner Voice will change your life, right from the beginning, the first time you act on it.

There is always one true Inner Voice. Trust it!

Gloria Steinem

Your Inner Voice in Action

*Specialize in handling
the big unknowns in your life.*

A home office-based catering business without food preparation was as inconceivable to my thinking mind as my Inner Voice's nudge to write the letter to a landlord I didn't know, requesting a two-bedroom apartment for myself and a man I had never met.

It is crucial to see there will always be unknowns as you honor the pull of your dreams and desires. Your Inner Whisper will give you an energetic nudge forward through the unknown, sometimes well before you are aware of the solution.

For your thinking mind, unknowns bring fear and confusion that usually result in a perceived dead end, unless you've gained the necessary daily skill of hearing, trusting, and acting on your Inner Voice.

New York City offers the most expensive chef-prepared food, ready and waiting in beautiful display cases that can quickly be delivered to a doorman, but also at the highest prices imaginable. I simply let my Inner Voice guide me to a clientele where cost was not a consideration. Most of these clients did not want a chef prepping food all day in their expensive kitchens and smelling up their apartment on the day of the event.

I became aware that my Inner Voice was pulling me to a catering business, delivering expensive food already prepared and ready to be heated and displayed on the client's beautiful dishes and served by my chef and staff.

Another essential variable to this successful Inner Voice-directed business was that I gained a reputation with my clients for having the best staff in New York City, which became a powerful referral engine.

> What unknown are you facing right now that feels overwhelming?
>
> What is your Inner Voice pulling you to do?

Chapter 5

The Importance of Your Inner Voice

Your Inner Voice is the most important part of who you are. Depend on it for every decision you make.

It is your truest compass. It stops you from making decisions based on outer appearances, which might include the input of others whether family members, friends, or business colleagues.

Your Inner Voice emboldens you to take the truest and bravest actions of your life—actions that your thinking mind would never allow you to consider.

Your Inner Voice is reflected in how you express yourself. You become more emotionally available in a conversation and more clearly set and vocalize your boundaries. You feel more at ease with expressing compassion, more comfortable with speaking from insight. You no longer resist expressing love. You give thanks freely, feeling and expressing gratitude more deeply than ever before. Voicing these truths keeps you present each day.

There are times when you will hear your Inner Voice strongly urging you to review situations in which you have given away your power or hurt someone by something you've said or done. It pushes you to rectify these situations.

Are you using your Inner Voice in your life?

Do you feel your Inner Voice pushing you to act on anything right now?

How are you being true to who you really are?

How might you be blocking your Inner Voice from providing insight into your truth?

The Spanish Villa and the GMC Yukon

One day in late spring 2001, I sat at the desk in my New York City apartment wrapping up my catering business affairs in preparation for a trip to Spain. In just two days, I would be visiting a friend with several homes around the world at her villa.

Her Inner Voice had prompted the invitation without any premeditation. Having met each other in a writing class three years earlier, we had become close friends, prompting her to invite me to a holiday dinner at her country house an hour outside of New York City.

During dinner, she heard herself asking me to visit her in Spain. I can still recall how she laughed in surprise, at that moment, when this invitation emerged from inside her, without any mental thought that she was even planning a trip to Spain. Her husband commented from across the table that he didn't realize that either. My Inner Voice would not let me say no.

Several weeks later, as my thinking mind pored over employee schedules, a feeling rose from inside me that I was supposed to buy a friend's GMC Yukon sitting in Montana. I immediately thought (above the neck), "What the hell is going on?"

I was so startled that I spoke out loud to the wall in front of me…"I don't need a car and haven't needed one in the fifteen years I've lived in New York City." Then I leaned back in my chair, took my arms off my desk, and stopped everything I was doing to listen to my Inner Voice.

I did not negate the importance of this outlandish thought flowing through me despite being so preoccupied with all my work. My thinking mind didn't see how I could afford to buy this car. But as I continued to build self-trust by honoring my Inner Voice's guidance, I didn't allow my thinking mind to harp on that thought any further. I chose, instead, to exercise trust in what it would have me do next now that it held my attention.

I felt directed to call my Montana friend. I recalled she had mentioned a month earlier that her Yukon was for sale. She bought a new car every few years, and there was always a waiting list of buyers eager to own her gently used cars because they were so beautifully maintained. She was a little startled when I immediately asked if she had sold the Yukon.

"It's really strange, but it hasn't sold," she said. "And this has never happened before."

I told her that I was being directed to buy it. She was confused, not sure she heard me right because she knew that I didn't need a vehicle in New York City. So, I said it again. And then she started to laugh at the realization that the car hadn't sold—because it had always been mine to buy!

This an example that higher assistance is always in alignment with what our Inner Voice is ready to place in our hands.

After our conversation, I walked over to the bank and, paying no heed to the chaotic thoughts in my thinking mind, filled out the paperwork for a car loan. Within two hours I was approved. Before the plane left the runway for Spain, I owned a GMC Yukon.

And yes, everything else in my office got done as well. It would be a year before I realized that buying this four-wheel-drive vehicle was an important step toward a future Inner Voice-fueled adventure in Montana!

If I didn't hear my Inner Voice, trusting it and acting on its guidance, then I wouldn't find myself receiving and accepting invitations to travel throughout the world or driving the cars just waiting for me to accept them.

Trust that your Inner Voice will lead you forward each day for the rest of your life and in the direction of your highest visions.

Nothing in life is more exciting and rewarding than the sudden flash of insight that leaves you a changed person.

Arthur Gordon Webster

Your Inner Voice in Action

> *Your Inner Voice is always working on your behalf,*
> *out in front of you, concerning your future.*

As I sat at the dinner table absorbing the invitation to Spain, my thinking mind immediately said I could not take an impulsive, last-minute, impromptu trip or spend money like this on a whim.

On the other hand, my Inner Voice reminded me that my friend was glamorous and fun and lived a global lifestyle, which would be a new experience and an incredible adventure without the cost of a hotel.

Sitting there, I felt an affirmation rolling up from deep inside me as my Inner Voice accepted the invite out of my smiling face.

My thinking mind had no power with its standard resistance. It knew that I had both the money and time to embrace this travel gift.

The situation of working at my desk and abruptly being nudged to buy the SUV was shocking. The long-term expense was unbelievable to my thinking mind… let alone the big question it raised on how this vehicle would fit into my life.

My thinking mind had no idea that my Inner Voice was working a year into my future with a connection to a property that would require a four-wheel drive.

There are two essential shifts here:

Our Inner Voice holds greater clarity regarding what, when, and how we spend money.

Our Inner Voice shows us that we can accept more than one good thing coming into our hands at the same time.

> Are you able to look back into your past to see how your thinking mind decisions have affected the results of your life today?
>
> Imagine your Inner Voice working out in front of you on your behalf for living your life forward!

Chapter 6

The Freedom of Your Inner Voice

There is sheer joy in the freedom you experience as you follow your Inner Voice's guidance. It is a freedom that adds dimension and color to your life, plus additional depth and meaning to your self-expression. Freedom comes into your life as soon as you begin to hear, trust, and act on your Inner Voice's guidance.

Look at your life. Be honest about where you aren't allowing yourself the freedom to live it your way. You may become aware that your needs have changed and no longer fit your lifestyle. New desires may bubble up from within you.

You may be directed to take time to hike on weekends. To accept the dog you've wanted for the past ten years. To become aware that you've felt for some time that you deserve a spa retreat. To know that you will stop using television as your relationship time with your loved one.

We aren't taught to keep freedom at the forefront of our life choices. Instead, our thinking mind overshadows what we know inside to be true for us.

Can you feel your Inner Voice as it pulls you to make changes in your life?

Are you trapped in your daily lifestyle and not honoring the inner knowing that pulls you to make the changes that will bring freedom?

Are you bogged down with debt because you don't hear your Inner Voice telling you that honoring your personal freedom should be the priority in your actions?

Ask yourself:

Is this more house than you need considering the house payment versus the additional free time and a reduced work schedule that you could enjoy by downsizing?

Is that car payment out of line with the car that meets your needs?

Is this career choice (or move) going to provide the freedom you desire or are you just taking the job because you need to pay the bills?

Can you see how your thinking mind and outer appearances got you into situations that do not create freedom?

Shifting below the neck and into your Inner Voice offers you the freedom to be emotionally available in your life and relationships. Now THAT is a freedom to experience! What in the heck would a world filled with emotionally available people look like? Wow!

Honoring your Inner Voice makes you free to transcend the need to meet others' expectations of you. For many people, this freedom alone would transform their lives.

The freedom that your Inner Voice offers for self-expression and personal signature is boundless. Think of that joy you have when you come across your favorite color expressed in the exact item for which you're shopping. Or the bliss you experience at the taste of your favorite dessert. Or the satisfaction of a cool glass of ice water that quenches an hour's worth of thirst.

This is the boundless energy that awaits you when you choose to hear, trust, and act on your Inner Voice's guidance.

Do not allow your thinking mind to persuade you that your Inner Voice-directed freedom is mere fantasy. The freedom you have when you live through your Inner Voice is REAL!

You will always know—no matter how subtle or powerful the feeling—when you are NOT honoring your Inner Voice:

You're spending time with people with whom you're bored or don't enjoy.

Your day is devoid of quiet time as you run helter-skelter from task to task.

You're comparing your ability to that of someone else.

You're dating someone with whom you feel unfulfilled.

Your Inner Voice has most likely been sending you red alerts in these situations for quite some time.

When you are connected to your Inner Voice and you act on its pull:

You are drawn toward and bring into your life those individuals who stimulate your creativity and add value to your life, as you do for them.

You give yourself the gift of quiet time to consider the truth of your Highest Visions and open your life wide to more expansive connections and opportunities.

You allow the self-expression that is you to come up from inside in all its creative power.

You are single but remain open to a life partner with whom you are a match, as your new partner will be with you.

Freedom will always result when we live from the inside out. When we begin to express what is true for us. There is no replacement for the feeling that comes from the freedom of expression.

Design the life that feels true for you and stand in the center of that freedom.

Sandals and a Suit

I was once the guest of a friend who lives an internationally mobile lifestyle. One night in Europe, as we were heading out for dinner, she suggested that I might be more comfortable if I wore sandals with my suits instead of the heavy, hot shoes I had brought with me. Now, I like to think that I'm teachable, and my intention is to be conscious. So, I implemented her suggestion when I returned to New York.

One evening I stopped at a bar after a business meeting wearing a beautiful suit and a new pair of handmade sandals. As I waited for a friend to meet me, a woman came over and introduced herself. She said that she represented a group of people in another area of the bar. Their attention had been drawn to the juxtaposition of my suit with the sandals, and they found the combination a terrific idea. The group wanted to know what I did for a living because their conservative firm would never allow the guys to wear something this dynamic!

I told her that I owned my company, so I didn't have to follow someone else's rules.

This episode has repeated itself many times over the years as my freedom to express myself activates people to tell me they aren't allowed to express themselves in such a manner in their workplace.

What is wrong with this picture? If self-expression is important to you, then where did you leave your packhorse? Load up and relocate your campsite!

While you're receiving your paycheck at your current post, apply to other firms and seek out new work environments where you can express your freedom. Keep the packhorse tied at your desk until you get the call to head 'em out!

Within a decade or so of exploring my freedom to wear sandals with a suit, I saw an ad for a company that specifically stated that it allowed employees the freedom to take a vacation whenever they wanted as long as they got their work done.

I realized that, finally, it seemed that "the times they were a-changing!"

As you hear, trust, and act from your Inner Voice's guidance, you will discover the freedom to be who you are and to accomplish what you came here to do.

On your way to accomplish greatness, you will hear a lot of noise. Listen to your Inner Voice and never let the distraction of the crowd discolor your poise.

Israelmore Ayivor

Your Inner Voice in Action

*Activating your self-expression
to match who you are inside*

When my friend suggested wearing sandals with my suits, I could feel her idea had struck pay dirt. My Inner Voice was immediately on a mission for expanded self-expression and creativity!

Turning New York City upside down to find the perfect sandal was indeed an Inner Whisper-directed treasure hunt. I eventually came across a handmade sandal with a price tag of $250.

I knew the simplicity, a loop over the big toe, a thin strap across my arch, and a lean, sculpted sole that was barely visible was the perfect juxtaposition for my expensive suits. I bought the sandals in three colors: black, skin tone, and muted violet.

This attire became my minimalist business expression, which I saw as one degree away from being barefoot and free while still in a suit and tie. I must confess that I also felt very confident, sophisticated, and upscale!

Once we stop playing by what others consider standard or following social dress codes that no longer "suit" us, it can become an invaluable rite-of-passage for raising the bar of what we wear to match our Inner Whisper.

There's no feeling like Inner Voice-directed dress for success specific to your pursuit of life!

This inner-directed self-expression will be a decisive factor in transcending the approval of others. They, instead, will be looking to you for direction.

> What creative self-expression nudges have you been feeling lately that are uniquely yours?

Chapter 7

The Power of Your Inner Voice

The power of that voice inside you knows no bounds.

While some people have yet to experience its full potential, many others don't realize the dormant power they can harness each day.

So, how in tune are you to act on a hunch, insight, or gut feeling? Until you connect with your Inner Voice, you're not!

You can't step into your Inner-Voice power and let it lead you forward until you are aware of it and willing to trust and act on it.

Let's look at some typical examples.

You awoke one morning KNOWING you should check on canceling a subscription. When you called, it was the last day of your billing month. Wow, you avoided being charged for another month!

You heeded an INSIGHT to reschedule an appointment without asking why. When you hung up the phone, it immediately rang, and your biggest client requested your presence at an urgent last-minute meeting.

You had a sudden HUNCH prompting you to check airline prices for an upcoming trip and then found the price had dropped two hundred dollars since yesterday. You booked your flight.

Consider water flowing through a garden-hose spray nozzle to visualize the power and the unique flow of Inner-Voice guidance coming up into your thinking mind each day. Your Inner Voice is best suited to tell your thinking mind to adjust the nozzle to spray an area, point the flow in a certain direction, and choose the volume of flow.

However, many of us erroneously rely on our thinking mind as it chooses to set its nozzle to spray in too narrow or too wide an area. We habitually point our energy flow in areas that do not require our attention (distractions) instead of those that best serve us. Or we allow it to choose too little or too strong a flow volume for the task at hand.

And then some of us find we have a big crimp in our hoses!

Your Inner Voice guides you with a threefold power: to adjust the thinking mind's nozzle settings throughout the day (its focus), to point it in the areas that need our attention (its direction), and to vary the amount flowing into the thinking mind needed to address those areas (its efforts).

Observe the individuals around you who may use this power at full volume or just halfway. Perhaps they have a kink or two in their hose. You can see it in the stress they carry, and in their faces locked in the grimace of survival mode. You can hear it in their angry, dissatisfied, self-absorbed, egotistical, thinking-mind conversations.

The level of dissatisfaction in our thinking minds and the power behind it is directly proportional to our resistance to that Inner Voice power ready and waiting to emerge from inside us. Fighting the flow within each of us is akin to fighting the flow of the universe that surrounds us. And THAT is a powerful energy current to oppose!

Why is it that we expend all this energy to fight the flow in ourselves…fighting what we know to be true, fighting our passions, and fighting what we want in our lives? In all instances, the answer is simple:

We are living above the neck in our thinking mind and basing our decisions on outer appearances.

We allow our thinking mind (ego) to believe that it is stronger, truer, or more powerful than our Inner Voice. We (our physical selves) become the losers in this battle every time. Witness the illness, addiction, and emotional pain around us… the rampant disease, financial problems, and loneliness that ensue when our thinking mind resists our unique energy flow.

Helping you to become consciously aware of your unique and powerful energy flow, as well as how your Inner Voice will help you to harness and apply it, is an important part of why I wrote *Your Brilliant Inner Whisper*.

Look around and you'll see people who allow their inner power to flow up through them. You can see it in how they creatively express themselves in their daily lives. You can see it in their lifestyles. Their inner power is reflected by everything in their life.

Little Caesar

I've worked more than a few jobs that my thinking mind chose as it overrode my Inner Voice's guidance to do otherwise.

It might have been the job title. Or the salary I thought I needed to pay bills. At times it was peer pressure. In all instances, I was living so far away from my truth and who I am that I would rationalize some reason for working in these positions.

I was justly rewarded with painful benefits including boredom, frustration, and dissatisfaction. My emotional pain from ignoring and dishonoring what I knew inside was true for me caused excessive physical and emotional wear and tear.

I would find some reason to bury my head in the sand or put on that lampshade to hide from what my inner self knew was not true in each circumstance. I would bind and gag its power until, finally, it was able to free itself and lead me out of the mess I had made.

Like many of us in our early twenties, I didn't know what career I wanted. My thinking mind rationalized that perhaps I could make a career out of my riding experience and knowledge of horses. I can still feel my skin beginning to crawl. Boy, was I in a body bag and ready for the morgue when I chose this ill-advised career track! Had I just dug a hole and buried myself, it would have cut out a lot of pain. Oh, I knew inside that it wasn't something I wanted to do, but because I was living above the neck, I couldn't devise anything else to generate income.

I applied for a job riding horses for a horse trainer who I had known since childhood on the show circuit despite having no real interest in working with horses in this way. The trainer was a little man with a big ego, a cruel streak, and a quick temper. I came to refer to him (behind his back, of course) as "Little Caesar."

My thinking mind (TM) ran the show as I ignored the bumping from my Inner Voice (IV). As I considered the job opportunity, the conversation between the two went something like this:

TM: "You must call up all the connections that you have and ask them for references. Tell them to call Little Caesar to recommend you directly for the job."

IV: "You really don't want this job; but okay, he already knows you and what you can do. Why are you doing all this needless extra work to sell yourself? He's lucky to have you."

TM: "The pay isn't much, but it will be a good experience… one that you need."

IV: "Huh? Come again? Didn't you decide that you were finished with horses other than as a hobby? So, what's with this good-experience sales pitch?"

TM: "Ignore the fact that you hate this job and that Little Caesar's actions demean you. You signed up for this, and you need the money that these long six-day weeks are bringing in."

IV: "Good Lord! At this rate, it'll be months before you get back on your real track with all this rationalization you're using to stay in the wrong job for the wrong reasons. How much longer must Little Caesar inflict emotional damage on you?"

Finally, I began to listen to my Inner Voice despite my thinking-mind machinations.

One day an urgent family obligation necessitated that I drive four hundred miles round-trip through the night after work. Little Caesar insisted that I be back at seven the next morning. During the drive, I realized that my Inner Voice had tolerated enough. Enough of Little Caesar's demeaning words and corrupt work ethics. Enough of my thinking mind's excuses to remain in that situation. Enough just to keep me awake to make the round-trip safe.

As I pulled into work early the next morning, I could FEEL that there had been a changing of the guard within me. Now that my Inner Voice was running the show, it tested a few ideas of choice phrasing out loud as I cleaned the first stall. I was surprised at how powerful it sounded, and for the first time since I started that job, I felt elated.

Little Caesar didn't know what hit him when he stuck his head in the barn that morning with his crooked grin asking, without any hint of compassion, if I was tired. My Inner Voice instantly brought him to hand, telling him to get busy with his own chores because I was finished as of that moment. I felt my legs kick into gear, and I walked out the door.

I remember being fully aware that Little Caesar was red-faced and hopping mad now that he was dealing with the power of my Inner Voice. And I felt so safe and protected at that moment. No one can argue with that power when you speak from the inside, even if they don't like it.

I understand now that Little Caesar didn't do anything to me. I was the one who had the crimp in my hose—living in my thinking mind. I had been less than truthful with myself when I justified taking that job.

Ask yourself right now about your current situation: "What am I thinking?" Or maybe you will recognize your "been there, done that" moment in a previous career decision. By living from our Inner Voice, we need never revisit this level of unconsciousness in future career decisions.

Our Inner Voice will always point us in a direction that fully supports who we are and what we came here to do. All we need do is hear, trust, and act on its wisdom.

The greatest of all miracles is that we need not be tomorrow what we are today. The greatest of all insights is that we cannot be tomorrow what we do not do today.

John C. Maxwell

Your Inner Voice in Action

Taking your stand to face what is not working in your life

I admit it took far too many months to stand up to myself in this unhappy work situation.

And, yes, I was unwilling to act on what was crystal clear to my thinking mind and Inner Voice…that I hated this situation!

The two reasons I continued to convince myself to stay were above-the-neck decisions:

I didn't want to tarnish the reputations of the people who had recommended me after they had stuck out their necks on my behalf.

I put off facing my problem because I had no idea what to do for a career or money to live on.

I now know that it's about taking an Inner Voice-directed stand with yourself on what you don't want. After this action, a new door will be revealed as the whisper within leads you forward.

> What action must you take on what is no longer a fit in your life today?

Chapter 8

The Strength of Your Inner Voice

Using your Inner Voice is like working out at the gym. The more you use it, the stronger it becomes. The more you use IT, the stronger YOU become. Both you and the people in your life will become aware of your increased inner strength. It is apparent in how you handle yourself, how you speak, and the way you make choices.

The growing strength of your Inner Voice is similar to the imperceptible changes to your muscles each time you lift weights. You may not realize your increased strength day by day until one day you suddenly lift a higher weight. Like the physical changes to your body, your Inner Voice's strength is felt and seen over time. You are building it from the inside out.

Your stronger Inner Voice may become apparent with a friend asking how you found the guts to make that (difficult) decision. Upon reflection, you realize the decision didn't appear daunting because you had grown accustomed to your inner strength.

At this point in my life, I make decisions from that place of inner strength. I'm not going on record to say that I have perfect (inner) washboard abs, mind you, but they are strong!

To write this book, I activated myself each day by saying three words: just—say—yes. Those words were my commitment to connect with my Inner Voice. Then I simply sat down at the computer and began to write. "Just—Say—Yes" gave me permission to step into the writing experience each day. Whenever I wanted to resist, I would say those three words again. Just—Say—Yes. Today it will be those three words. Tomorrow it will be those three words. Just—Say—Yes is the mantra rooted deep inside me now.

That mantra helped me to cross the invisible line of my resistance every time. Those words quieted my thinking mind and its familiar continuous loop of self-deprecating banter:

"You're not a writer; you don't know what you're doing; you're a hit-or-miss speller; you aren't strong at grammar; you couldn't edit your way out of a revolving door; you don't have enough stories for each chapter; you can't make it through all the days of isolation or the emotional dredging of your guts; your Inner Voice will never give you enough material to fill the chapters; you'll never get an agent; you'll never get published…."

All thinking mind loops wreak havoc. That is why it is so important to Just—Say—Yes in those moments and drop below the neck again. That is where your answers and your peace await you.

The Victory Arch

I'm fascinated by the Arc de Triomphe in Paris. An immense edifice commissioned by Napoleon to honor his Austerlitz victory, it has come to represent the celebration of all French victories. It is so large that a biplane once flew through it. Talk about a monument to overcoming the "NOs" of adversity!

Some of my biggest life victories have come from the NOs I have confronted.

At first glance, these NOs (as in "no way through") appeared impenetrable and overwhelming. NO, I won't survive this. NO, I can't face this. NO, this is too big for me. They seemed to be insurmountable obstacles in my life's path:

I can't make it as a singer in New York. NO!

I have to tell my family and friends that I'm Gay. NO!

I have been diagnosed with cancer. NO!

I am being pulled to write. NO!

My thinking mind saw only impenetrable barriers that lacked openings at their centers through which I could reach my YES. But through the years, I have come to trust my Inner Voice to lead me forward through each of these false barriers.

Each NO has had at its center a victory arch through which I trusted myself to walk into the YES of who I am.

Each victory is a testimony to the strength of my Inner Voice as I went further below the neck and farther away from the NOs in my thinking mind.

The NO in my singing career meant facing that it was over. The money supporting my efforts was gone. The years of hard work and diligence felt wasted. I stood in front of what appeared to be a solid NO—the painful question of how I would ever begin to start over.

The NO in admitting that I am Gay also appeared impenetrable. It made Mount Everest look like a pimple! Life as I knew it suddenly disappeared. I didn't want to be different from everyone in my life. I didn't want to go through this experience that was dead center in my life path.

The NO in my cancer diagnosis was different than you might imagine. The pain of the NO wasn't that I might die; rather, it was that I had to face personal changes that I didn't want to make. I had to stop eating everything I liked with refined sugar. NO! Stop drinking anything acidic—like coffee and red wine. NO!

And the NO that stood solidly in the way of my writing was the thought of having to get back on the horse. It just seemed too hard, too emotional, and too isolated. NO! Out of the question!

Each of you has your NOs.

I'm not happy in my marriage.

I'm bankrupt.

I can't express my feelings.

I'm in a career that I hate.

I'm ashamed of where my life is going.

I'm not emotionally available.

I'm scared of intimacy.

I'm flunking out of school and I can't tell my parents.

Why do our perceived barriers activate such strong NO's?

We don't want to leave the herd mentality and face our unique life path.

We don't want to be shunned or gossiped about for being different.

We don't want to become an entrepreneur to create a life that's true for us.

We don't want to see our personal fears and issues smack in our faces.

We don't want to do our individual work.

We don't want to see the end of our life.

We don't want to take responsibility for being consciously aware.

We don't want to face the fork in the road that we can't see beyond.

From the NO in our lives, we must pass through the center of our victory arch to stand in the YES on the other side.

Through the NO in my singing career, I was lucky to work with some of the top singing and performing coaches in the world. I can't imagine never having experienced living in New York City. It has been one of the most important springboards to who I am today. YES, victory!

Through the NO of facing my being Gay, I have passed through the most important victory arch of my life walk. Being different has allowed me to develop a level of inner trust that few people experience. This trust has opened up my life. I write with an Inner-Voice confidence that doesn't need approval. YES, victory!

Through the NO of my cancer diagnosis, I see each day as a dance. It's about changes that I need to make anyway. It's not about fear. It's not about how long I have to live. It's about facing me. It's about trusting me. The diagnosis isn't about cancer. It's about becoming consciously aware of what's lying underneath that I need to address. YES, victory!

Through the NO of being called to write, I am living an adventure that I never expected. As I review my writing, my thinking mind can't believe what I have found inside myself. What if I hadn't passed through my victory arch in the "NO, I don't want to try writing"? I would have missed the "YES, Victory!" of the writer inside of me.

In the words of Steve Jobs, "Your time is limited, so don't waste it living someone else's life. Have the courage to follow your heart and intuition. They somehow already know what you truly want to become."

I encourage you to write down four of your NOs and then walk through the invisible arches of each one to the YES of who you are on the other side. Trust your Inner Voice to pull you through what only APPEARS to be an impenetrable NO. You will find your victory arch in the YES that awaits you on the other side.

◇◇◇◇◇◇◇◇◇◇◇◇◇◇◇◇◇◇◇◇◇◇◇◇◇◇◇◇◇◇◇◇◇◇◇◇◇◇◇

Let your Inner Voice guide you from the NO in your thinking mind—through your Arc de Triomphe— to the YES that awaits you on the other side.

◇◇◇◇◇◇◇◇◇◇◇◇◇◇◇◇◇◇◇◇◇◇◇◇◇◇◇◇◇◇◇◇◇◇◇◇◇◇◇

People may doubt you,
but never doubt your deep inner call,
Inner Voice, inner strength.

Amit Ray

Your Inner Voice in Action

> *The size of your NO is directly proportional to the YES in your success.*

I am only choosing one of my four NOs for this review.

My life continues on eight years beyond saying YES to my cancer. Back when I was diagnosed with a slow-growing carcinoid cancer, I made a choice not to take the monthly two-thousand-dollar shot to impede the cancer's development.

Instead, I chose to go alkaline because a friend told me that cancer doesn't grow in an alkaline environment. I didn't realize staying alkaline would not work for me because of my blood sugar fluctuation due to my diabetes.

Around the time of this realization, I entered a five-year period where my life became busy, and I put my cancer on the back burner. Also, during this phase, I left New York City and landed in Oregon.

After arriving in the Pacific Northwest, my Inner Voice pushed me to check on my cancer. My general practitioner and an oncologist both verified the cancer had grown. They also told me I was lucky because one of the world's leading doctors for my type of cancer was in Portland, Oregon, only a five-hour drive away.

The Portland doctor performed surgery on my liver cancer and removed forty percent. Twelve months later, my doctor included me in the first group of Americans to access a new drug from Italy for this type of cancer. My cancer has not grown in the two years since taking this drug.

There's glaring higher assistance and divine scheduling with me stopping in Oregon when I had always planned to move to California. Therefore, I had easy access to this cancer specialist in Portland.

Another powerful sign that my higher assistance was in full force: the week I drove to Portland for my doctor's appointment, the FDA approved the new Italian drug, which I would be included to receive a year later.

Saying YES to my cancer has worked for me. I must share that I believe that I chose this cancer, on a soul level, as part of my learning in this lifetime.

I have come to understand the size of the NO is directly proportional to the power of the YES, and our Inner Voice always rises to the occasion to pull us right through our NOs to our YESs.

> What are four NOs you have related to scary outer appearances?
>
> After writing these down, are you aware of the YESs nudging you forward with the perfect actions to take?

Chapter 9

Becoming Aware of Your Inner Voice

You must first choose to become aware of your Inner Voice before you begin to effectively utilize its power in your daily life. Believe me, it's worth the effort.

So, whether or not you are fully on board one-hundred percent, let's just step into it from wherever you are right now. Hang on and take one step forward, saying the following aloud:

"I am now aware that I have an Inner Voice that can guide my life."

Congratulations, it's that easy!

You have made your verbal commitment to honor its guidance. Now, just go on with your day.

Starting today and in the days and weeks to come, write down in a notebook or journal ALL the thoughts that come up into your thinking mind. Yes, each one—no matter how "trivial" you perceive that thought. Most of these thoughts will be "to-do" items that require some sort of follow-through effort.

It might be a thought out of nowhere to call a friend this afternoon... to pick up more Kleenex when you head out from work at the day's end... to make an appointment for an oil change ... switch to a more economical calling plan, or upgrade your AAA card to a Gold membership in case you take an extended road trip. It doesn't matter how small or insignificant the thought is. WRITE IT DOWN.

If some of these "to-do's" can be handled with a phone call right now, I encourage you to do it, or as soon as you have the time. Attending to these quickly frees you up.

Give no further thought (the how and why) to these "to-dos" that you write down. Just be aware of them as they flow up into your thinking mind. Write them down (or quickly handle them) and then let them go.

Each of these written thoughts has unique energy associated with it. You will come to see the importance of letting that energy be guided by your Inner Voice to show you the order that you will address each "to-do" now or in the days or months to come. Do not allow your thinking mind to decide which order that it wants to attend to them.

It's easier to become aware of your Inner Voice if you start with the everyday errands. The key is to stay consciously aware. In the past, you might have just rushed through them without recognizing the value of this process of following an energetic pull. Learn to feel the activation from the flow as your Inner Voice starts to lead you.

In the past, where your thinking mind wanted to control or judge each thought that showed itself, creating a bottleneck that blocked the flow, it will now start to allow these "to-dos" to pass right through it.

You are now starting to say YES to your inner flow.

Your thinking mind will soon yield to your Inner Voice; it will no longer sit like a boulder in the middle of a stream forcing everything to flow around it. No longer will control or judgment stemming from the thinking mind impede your decision to act on those "to-dos."

Once you commit to honor the flow of your "to-dos," you will become more consciously aware of your daily actions. You might be driving down the highway and find you're suddenly aware that you like a certain vehicle grill. Or that you are now attracted to a building that you have passed five days a week for two years and never thought about until now.

You might suddenly become aware of a desire to buy flowers for your spouse, a feeling that came up in you out of nowhere, without reason. You could suddenly become aware of thinking of your pet or a friend in the middle of a conference call.

You DO NOT need to know what each thought is about in these unexpected moments.

You DO need to be aware that these unexpected thoughts ARE happening and that they can lead you forward to create a life that fits you. They are pieces of your life-flow energy that will fit together in time. The process is not about busyness; it is about preparing you to shift.

As you shift into conscious awareness, so too will the matters about which you become conscious begin to shift. You may suddenly become aware of a feeling that you need to change your evening schedule without the slightest clue as to why. NOW is where you will see the proof as you honor the feeling and change your schedule, acting and trusting your Inner Voice.

Being consciously aware could reunite you with someone you haven't seen in twenty years who unexpectedly stopped by your house… and who you would·have missed had you proceeded with your original schedule. Remain aware of the flow of these feelings (energy connected to thought) that emerge to alter your plans, your direction, or a prior commitment. The process is preparing you for those life-altering milestones in the future.

Becoming consciously aware of what you like is an added benefit as you gain experience in connecting comfortably with your Inner Voice. You will notice the things you like reflect their unique energy in addition to those that you no longer prefer.

This will become an important distinction, especially when you become consciously aware of the energy you dislike and realize that you have carried it far too long.

The Invisible Line

My deep involvement with horses set the stage for my early recognition of that certain "something" going on inside of me, which I would later come to know as my Inner Voice.

At fourteen I was still a beginning horse competitor, though I had taken quite a few lessons. I lacked confidence and was certainly not very self-aware at this stage. I perceived at the time that most of the other kids had "more"—talent, experience, and fancier horses. I was the average kid who felt overwhelmed by outer appearances.

During one horse competition, however, I realized as I exited the ring that I couldn't remember any of it happening. Not one bit. Everything seemed to be a blur. It had gone so fast.

Suddenly I heard my name over the loudspeaker. I had won!

I was confused and shocked. A fellow competitor I barely knew remarked, "It's about time you started winning."

I said incredulously, "I can't believe I won."

She laughed and replied, "You had a better go than the rest of us and you deserved the win."

I had a better go? I couldn't remember anything about my performance! It was then that I sensed I had crossed an invisible line. Something inside of me had performed the routine. I had not been in my (thinking) mind at all.

I was too young and unaware to realize that I had gone below the neck and allowed my Inner Voice to take over during the performance. At most, I recognized that invisible line. The rest was… well, you know… invisible.

About three years and numerous horse competitions later, I had made the final cut out of fifty-five competitors and was in the middle of performing my routine. My horse moved at a smooth gallop. I was focused only on staying out of trouble with the other horses and contestants around me.

As I rounded the corner at the end of the arena, suddenly everything stood still, frozen at that moment.

I remember facing the audience in the stands, and I can still tell you, thirty years later, the names associated with each friendly face. In that moment, rising up from inside of me, came a feeling that I had won the competition even though I was only halfway through it.

The next thing I became aware of was my horse still loping along, having made the turn. I had already almost reached the other end of the arena.

Later, I sat in the line-up listening to the placings being announced… "In sixth place… fifth, fourth, third, second …" I felt that exhilarating chill come up from inside when I was announced as the winner. While I was still too young to have explained or described the power of my inner awareness at that moment, it became clear that something inside me had definitely made itself known.

These are two early examples of feeling a power inside of me before I had a name for it. Before I ever believed it was anything. Before I understood it. Before I could describe it. And way before I would use its power to guide me. But I felt it, and I never forgot the truth of that feeling.

Only years later would I become familiar with the phrase "Inner Voice" as I began to understand its value and importance as a tool to direct my life.

Connecting with Inner Voice energy is like learning to ride a bicycle at that moment when you find the connection between your inner and outer balance. You are aware of the shift because you have crossed an invisible line where the within and the without are balanced. No more need for training wheels!

Rather than asking "how" or "why," go below the neck and trust Your Inner Voice's guidance. It will always lead you forward.

Discovery is the journey; insight is the destination.

Gary Hamel

Your Inner Voice in Action

*An invisible line presents itself to you
every day of your life.*

The invisible line is where most of the herd stops: the masses, those willing to settle for less, people with a need to fit in or choosing to stay average, those resisting their inner nudge to act on their desires because they don't want to act beyond their comfort zone.

They remain above the neck instead of letting the pull of the whisper of their Inner Voice reveal the way forward.

The invisible line lies between the outer appearances and the energetic nudge of your Inner Voice to action. The invisible line is immediately behind you when you act on the whisper within.

The upgrade from the invisible line in my youth—winning the class but not remembering my actions—has become an upgraded awareness of acting on the Inner Whisper's pull in the present moment.

It is also essential to become aware there is a knowingness that accompanies the Inner Voice… like my awareness on the turn in the arena telling me I had won the class.

Your Inner Voice allows you to embrace your life as an ever-present expanding gift!

> Looking back, can you recall a time you crossed the invisible line to a success you didn't expect?

Chapter 10

Hearing Your Inner Voice

Inner Voice is energy. It is a feeling. It is a knowing. It is an awareness.

The first step in hearing your Inner Voice is to honor the feeling that suddenly (or sometimes slowly) comes up through you. As you do, you will come to accept this knowing that is ready to show you something... leading you to do something or making you aware in ways you hadn't been a few moments earlier.

There will be times you won't know where that first step is taking you: making a phone call without having a clue as to what the conversation will be about; experiencing a sudden feeling to take the next left turn or to pull over for a few minutes; feeling an urge to choose an alternate route for no apparent reason.

Try it just for fun. You're not hurting anyone, right? I promise you it's not painful!

Hearing your Inner Voice as it prompts you to follow these simple steps will prepare you for those future life-altering moments when you are fully consciously aware and act in ways that will bring you closer to who you are.

It could start with you suddenly feeling directed to invite three people over for dinner and you don't have any idea why you called them or what you'll be serving. It could well be that they are not supposed to be available to accept your offer because it is not about dinner. Your Inner Voice could be directing you to connect with each of them for a specific reason that will be revealed to you in those conversations. You simply need to acknowledge the urge and proceed with each call.

When taking your first steps, it is not about putting yourself at risk. In fact, the only risk that your Inner Voice will ever offer is that you will break through to who you are and what you came here to do. It will never place you or others in harm's way.

Rather, these simple exercises in hearing your Inner Voice are about spreading your wings so you act in ways that feel right to you. This will empower you to honor the feelings connected to the thoughts you are becoming consciously aware of.

They come from a place of inner love and trust. You'll know them when you feel them.

Consider this exercise: buy a gift for a loved one to practice hearing your Inner Voice. It can feel uncomfortable for some of us to face how unattached we are when buying gifts.

So, step into your commitment to become consciously aware of your feelings as you make your way through a gift purchase. Your awareness is heightened by following and honoring Inner Voice energy. You need not have any thinking-mind tension… because a gift can easily be exchanged!

Your daily wardrobe decisions are another simple exercise to become consciously aware of and honor your Inner Voice's direction. I now only wear clothes that reflect the energy of the inner me and honor this direction every day. You too can benefit from practicing this daily awareness.

One of the more exhilarating exercises to practice hearing your Inner Voice is to take a road trip scheduled only through your inner guidance: when to drive, where to stay, and impromptu route changes.

Stop to spend time along the way only as you feel directed. Your inner guidance may influence the course of your trip for a variety of divine reasons: joy, protection, scheduling, or less stress. You will experience everything that is divinely intended once you learn to get out of your thinking mind and go below the neck. That is where you will begin to hear your Inner Voice.

Have fun! Knock yourself (from the inside) out!

What was your first encounter with your Inner Voice? Maybe you're not sure if you've experienced one yet.

Let's take a look at my first encounter with the Inner Whisper, which can help you. Becoming aware of my Inner Voice for the first time was a serious shock to my system, one that I hope to alleviate in you through these stories.

The First Time I Heard My Inner Whisper

It began early one morning in my sophomore year of college as I walked on my way to class. Suddenly, I experienced an overwhelming emotional energy that literally exploded inside and moved up through me into my thinking mind.

It was accompanied by a thought that caught me completely by surprise. My thinking mind was stunned.

The burst of energy connected to this feeling/thought told me to quit my classes and simply ski for the rest of the college quarter! I was confused and shaken, now aware of this powerful inner feeling out of nowhere. What the heck just happened inside of me? I had been fine five steps earlier! I had never felt anything this emotionally overwhelming ever before.

Quit my classes? Ski for the rest of the quarter? My dad would kick my butt!

I was being pushed to reject everything my parents, upbringing, and schooling had taught me about following the rules. In those moments, I didn't know that this turn of events was my Inner Voice speaking to me. It was just this "thing" that happened inside of me that I couldn't deny. Couldn't explain. And yet somehow, I knew that it was real.

I sat on a bench trying to figure out what had just happened. I next became aware of trying to understand why no one had ever mentioned this powerful voice that was inside of me.

Why wasn't I given any tools to prepare for this moment?

Why was there no previous guidance from my parents or teachers to prepare me for the day that this voice inside would make itself known to me? No one had ever sat me down and told me this fact!

My thinking mind yelled at full volume, "No, don't do it! This feeling inside you isn't real! Why would you do something that no one around you would conceive of doing? What will your dad think?"

While my thinking mind continued to tell me that this inner feeling couldn't be real, the powerful voice inside of me did not rest. It kept pushing me with a thought/feeling to chuck my father's money that I had just used to pay for the semester two days earlier.

Here I was in a situation that I could not explain, justify, or dare seek advice for. Yet at that moment, I knew whatever was happening inside of me was pivotal; my father's needs were no longer my priority. His feelings were no longer more important than what I felt inside.

It was simply about me somehow mustering the guts and the strength to listen to and trust the inner me.

Then a feeling arose that the money wasn't being thrown away. Rather, it was paving the way for an experience that the inner me knew was part of my true learning. It would be a lesson that would influence all my future decisions.

So, I did it! I quit all my classes and didn't tell my father. Despite the deep fear of where my actions might lead, something inside pulled me forward to ski every day. It was my first true leap of inner trust.

It was only years later that I came to see how this moment was connected to the center thread of my life path. Though I didn't know back then, part of the center thread of that pivotal moment was tied to my writing this book.

In retrospect, it represented my first significant step into who I am. It was a conscious decision to let the energy and "knowing" to act on a feeling connected to a thought lead the way. It was in a direction away from the outer appearances and rationale of my thinking mind.

◇◇

Your choice to hear your Inner Voice's guidance may be the fork-in-the-road moment that will lead you to discover who you are and what you came here to do.

◇◇

Be aware of your Inner Voice and follow it, though most of the time it will tell you the most uncomfortable path to choose.

Glenn Close

Your Inner Voice in Action

*Everything is in place to take
inner-directed forks on your life path.*

Choosing to quit my classes was the first real stand I had ever taken with myself, which redirected my life toward who I was inside and away from all the rules I had been trained to follow.

Though having no preparation for this defining fork-in-the-road event, an undeniable clarity and energetic pull were real. I had not accessed this inner level of awareness before this moment.

The higher assistance at work here was that by paying my fees, I had a place to eat and live in the dorm and a student season ski pass. So, everything was in place for me to honor my Inner-Voice-directed ski schooling.

It can be helpful to see each of these forks in the road as decisions directed from a deep soul level.

This college decision to trust my inner self above all else, therefore honoring a nudge to quit my classes and ski, transitioned me into a one-day-at-a-time trust that continues today. It can be a powerful rhythm for living your life.

What is your version of quitting classes and going skiing that your Inner Voice is calling you to take?

Can you see how everything is in place for this life fork?

Chapter 11

Trusting your Inner Voice

Trusting your Inner Voice is a continual building process, brick by brick, moment to moment, that eventually creates a solid foundation and structure on which you can rely. It serves as a powerful catalyst to activate your conscious awareness. Trust results from acting on your Inner Voice's guidance. It is a vital key that will help open the doors to who you are and what you came here to do.

Trust is NOT outside of you. Rather, it begins deep within you and is developed through practice. Have no worries if you currently feel unable to trust either yourself or others. This is simply your thinking mind second-guessing your Inner Voice. Once you learn to trust your Inner Voice, you need never wonder about trusting anyone else but YOU!

Trust-based (Inner Voice) decisions are lessons that free us to move forward, at ease with our past actions. They don't carry self-doubt, even if they don't work out in the way we expected in our thinking minds.

We know that we are living from a place of trust within and from our Inner Voice when we take full ownership and responsibility for the past decisions we made that (seemingly) did not work out as we anticipated they would.

Inner-Voice trust is an energetic cord tied to powerful dreams rooted deep within us. It allows us to know that our dreams are real.

Any lack of connection to our dreams and trust in our Inner Voice is apparent when we find ourselves looking across the fence at someone else's perceived easier path or greener pastures. Standing in the trust of our Inner Voice, we know we will manifest what is true for us in our own backyard. It is never about what lies across the fence. Rather, it's always about staying below the neck and out of the thinking mind.

There is a vast difference between thinking-mind lack ("Where's mine?") and Inner-Voice supply ("It has my name on it.").

When you become consciously aware of a feeling connected to a thought that is true for you, at that moment you must trust yourself, owning that it is real and true enough for you to act upon.

For example, if you are directed from inside to purchase a special item, you must trust that feeling connected to a thought and act upon it, knowing that you will be shown every step of the way forward.

Through each step, the actions you take bring you to even deeper levels of trust. If you are directed from inside to purchase a home or a car or a new outfit, and act on your inner knowing, then you have gained experience in trusting yourself.

You are trusting that you will be shown every step of the way forward—the money to purchase the house, the divinely perfect car, the right occasion tied to the new outfit—or you would not have felt the direction to purchase it.

Actions based on Inner-Voice trust bring us closer to living our lives from the place of who we are.

A Leap of Trust

The dark bank of clouds seemed to suddenly materialize as I rushed along the creek looking for a crossing. As the rain started, I knew my time was up.

I had two choices: trust my fancy three-year-old colt, Classy Cadet, to make a jump that most horses couldn't or wouldn't attempt or backtrack forty-five minutes through soil that would quickly turn into bog holes I couldn't see. The possibility of him pulling a tendon forced me through my mental fear to an inner decision.

At sixteen I wasn't aware of the term Inner Voice, but in that moment and despite my fear, something inside of me trusted that he could make this jump. And I knew if I didn't get to my trailer soon, I would never be able to drive through a muddy three-mile road.

I had been riding Cadet for the past six months. He had been raised in these hills and was familiar with the terrain. Smart and athletic, he was more horsepower than anything I had ever owned or ridden. More than one person told me that I had bought the horse of a lifetime.

But the quality that made Cadet special was his willingness to try anything that was asked of him.

As I showed him the edge of the bank, he snorted and jumped sideways. I found a spot with a slight downhill slope that aided my takeoff, with flat terrain directly across on the other bank. Showing Cadet the edge a second time, he snorted and tried to dance sideways, but I held him until he stood still.

Trotting away and deciding on the distance for my final approach, I hoped he sensed the idea of what I was going to ask him to do. I was in turmoil about the best speed going into the bank. Should I come in at a fast trot to make sure his feet would be in a good position for takeoff? Or come in at a gallop for added momentum?

I held his head tight with one rein in each hand to keep him moving straight for the bank's edge. As we came forward at a strong trot, I increased our speed the closer we got to the edge. I still remember feeling the knot in my stomach as I drove him forward with my legs.

I was caught off guard as he suddenly leaped into the air and his neck hit me in the face, blinding me with pain. My shirt hooked on the saddle horn and stopped me from falling off as his back feet left the ground. My only memory during the jump is of pain and trying to hang on.

My ribcage came down on the saddle horn from the impact of his front feet landing on the far bank. My shirt tore as I was thrown back into the seat of my saddle as one hind foot struck solid ground. Then my saddle dropped down as his other foot slipped back over the edge of the bank. Cadet groaned and strained forward, somehow pulling us onto the bank.

As I slid down from the saddle, holding my ribs and trying to regain my breath, I knew I had to keep him walking in a circle. Blinking through the tears of the pain in my forehead and nose, I tried to see if he was limping as the rain began to fall harder.

Suddenly the horse stopped, shook his whole body, and started bobbing his head in reaction to the rain. It was as if to say, "Get me in that trailer and let's get out of here." I stiffly climbed back on and we headed for the truck, and soon we made our way home.

Years later, when Cadet and I were ranked nationally as one of the ten best teams in working cattle, I finally understood the distance his willingness had carried me on that jump. Many times since his passing, I would have given anything for his partnership on my own life jumps. Yes, he was the horse of a lifetime.

I trusted my Inner Voice that day way before I knew what it was or had a name for it. I share this story to remind each of you that we always have the inner push before we're aware of its powerful guidance in our lives.

NOW is the time to trust your Inner Voice.
You need never second-guess yourself again.

Always listen to your Inner Voice.

Oprah

Your Inner Voice in Action

*There is always inner knowing
accompanying a life leap.*

The creek bank was about choosing to trust my inner knowing on this incredible horse.

My Inner Whisper was clear that I didn't dare let outer appearances or consequences override this knowing inside.

Looking back, I am aware the higher assistance around me and my horse would not have let me take this leap if it wasn't right.

Access to my inner knowing that day is now a regular touchstone for my life leaps and continues to be my most trustworthy gauge for each situation.

The strength gained in trusting this leap to the other bank is no different from the jump to start writing this book, even though I had never planned or prepared to be a writer. It's always about the knowing inside directly tied to the leap forward.

The jump with my horse was my first experience of choosing to do the job immediately at hand, from a directed action inside of me.

This leap also helped prepare me to trust myself on a whole new level to make life leaps far into my future.

> What is one leap that you know you must make today?

Chapter 12

Acting on Your Inner Voice

Your life will take on an entirely new dimension when you begin to act on the guidance of your Inner Voice.

In the past, we have stopped short when we followed a hunch only so far or acknowledged but then ignored a gut feeling. Or when we only talked about an insight without acting on it.

Don't blame yourself. Many of us lacked role models that would have inspired us to act on the guidance of our Inner Voice. No one taught us about its powerful place in our lives or that it even existed. But now, through the pages of *Your Brilliant Inner Whisper*, you can learn to hear, trust, and act on it.

I can imagine your thinking mind saying right now, "What if I tried it and didn't work out?"

Look around you and see how much *hasn't* worked out in your life while you have ignored your Inner Voice!

Jumping into action can seem like a major leap, but just take one step forward at a time. It won't be long before acting from your inner wisdom adds an exciting element to your life. It adds a whole new dimension to living. It involves an unknown part of you that will start to feel so right.

Acting on my Inner Voice is now an important part of each day. It has come to feel natural, as it will for you. It has proven itself in many ways, and I have grown to trust it implicitly.

People in your life will begin to notice changes in you and the actions you take. They may be affected directly or through their observations of your process. Your actions will catch their attention because you are living from the truest part of yourself.

Have fun with this process and do not be concerned with the effects your transformation may have on your peers. You are now their teacher. They have their process too and, in many cases, you will be activating them to step into their truth. Their Inner Voice might activate them to move forward with you or take them on a path of their own even if it's out of your life.

It is also important to understand that when you hear, trust, and act on your Inner Voice's guidance, you are directly connected to your highest visions.

That's right. You are no longer separated from those dreams that retreated deep inside you when you acted from the realm of limitation in your thinking mind when it told you that your goals were impossible.

Don't worry; they're still alive and well. With your thinking mind out of the way, you will feel more powerfully connected to them than ever before. You can and will attain your highest visions when you follow your Inner Voice.

Run and Turn in a Natural Way

In my early years working with horses and entering riding competitions, I became aware that a vital training component was to let them run and turn in a way that is natural for them. I offered direction and guidance, but I had to first become consciously aware of the natural way that the horse chose to move and act on what I asked it to do. Each horse was different, and I would listen for my inner guidance—that feeling that would emerge from within—to determine the best course to work together.

Likewise, My Inner Voice pulls me forward to run and turn in a way that is natural for me. I act on its guidance despite my thinking mind being surprised at times by the blind curves that appear on my path.

These "twisty-turny" parts can seem intimidating and overwhelming despite the trust I have in my Inner Voice's guidance.

When I lived in New York, my Inner Voice pushed me to mail a deposit for a puppy that had not yet been born… and I lived in a building that didn't allow dogs! Talk about a twisty-turny part! What was my Inner Voice up to?

Over the past several years, my Inner Voice had occasionally revealed to me that a miniature Australian Shepherd would accompany me as part of the talks and workshops associated with *Your Brilliant Inner Whisper*. Four months before completing this book, my Inner Voice pulled me to begin searching Australian Shepherd websites all over the country to educate myself. But I never knew why or when the puppy might appear, much less how I would have it given my lifestyle. My thinking mind told me that I wasn't ready yet.

But once I mailed the nonrefundable deposit, I became consciously aware that what had to shift to bring the puppy into my reality was ME! Since my building didn't accept dogs, I would be leaving my apartment in New York after twenty-five-plus years. What?!

In these moments, my thinking mind races with all its limiting thoughts based on the outer appearances. Where will I go? Why give up a rent-free lifestyle? How am I going to care for a puppy with my schedule? Now I simply stay below the neck, trusting that my Inner Voice will pull me forward through the twisty-turny parts. I also remain consciously aware of signs that validate my trust.

Within minutes of finalizing the layout for the initial publication of *Your Brilliant Inner Whisper*, I was notified that my puppy "Razz" had been born.

The act of sending the puppy deposit fully committed me to take *Your Brilliant Inner Whisper* out into the world. I was no longer able to cling to my apartment, neighborhood, or lifestyle. My Inner Voice showed me that I was ready to move forward, regardless of what my thinking mind told me.

Don't ever expect your Inner Voice to allow you to run and turn in familiar ways!

And the twisty-turny part continues.

After years of the fast-paced responsibility of owning a successful catering business, I was ready to leave New York with the intention of eventually ending up in the warm weather of California.

This transition to a slower pace included honoring the inner nudge to purchase a miniature Australian Shepherd puppy. I started looking online at breeders all over the country and found one in Tucson, Arizona.

A rural setting for a few months before leaving the East Coast would be great for us to play while I finished things in New York City.

As I was preparing to publish the initial version of *Your Brilliant Inner Whisper*, my Inner Voice guided me to consider winter cottage rentals near the Connecticut shore. I wanted a beach setting for Razz and me to bond and explore while I was winding down my catering business. This rental house would become my base to launch my initial book while I cleared out my New York apartment.

Acting further on the guidance of my Inner Voice, I also purchased a flight from New York to Tucson to pick up Razz, and then one back to Hartford, Connecticut. This rental would become our home until we finally left the East Coast to zigzag our way west to Oregon.

Three weeks after purchasing my tickets, I signed a lease on a beautiful four-bedroom one block from the water. Now Razz and I would start our daily adventure with a play date running on the beach each morning.

My Inner Voice unerringly guided me to wonderful locations, whether a block from Central Park or the waterfront of Connecticut. This supply was always the result of Inner-Voice-directed trust and action through the twisty-turny parts to the perfect location.

Your Inner Voice will pull you to run and turn in a way that is natural for YOU. It will pull you through the twisty-turny parts as it guides you forward on your unique path.

*In the silence, you hear the truth
and know the solution.
Listen to the Inner Voice within.*

Deepak Chopra

EREC LINDBERG

Your Inner Voice in Action

> *The pursuit of your dreams is
> what your Inner Voice specializes in.*

My awareness of how a horse wants to run and turn in a natural way has become a blueprint for living my own life.

Trusting my Inner Whisper frees me up to allow myself to run and turn in a natural alignment with the energetic pull of my dreams and desires.

Purchasing three flights to a distant airport halfway around the country and before I had a signed lease on a home could only be faced with the guidance of my Inner Voice.

In this situation, running and turning in a way that was natural meant I had to trust the Inner Whisper to make all three connecting flights, two of which had very tight plane changes while hauling a puppy and carrier.

I had trusted my inner direction when purchasing these flights, so I knew they would be handled in divine scheduling.

The lease didn't start until ten days after our Connecticut arrival, so we slept on the living room floor of my cousin's small house. I felt immense gratitude that first night sitting by the fire in our two-story colonial. It was wonderful to climb into a bed again!

You will know if it's time to commit to your own version of a "puppy deposit," which means there's no turning back.

Is it time to book your life version of flights and landings to unknown destinations directed by the pull from within?

And remember, it is not about expecting your Inner Voice to run and turn in a familiar way!

> What are you ready to let go of so you can run toward the pull of your dreams and desires?

Chapter 13

Living with and from Your Inner Voice

It is said that early tribesmen had a connection to the earth and their surroundings based on something other than the spoken word. Rather, they knew that they would be led to the animals and food they needed to survive. This unspoken connection has been described as an "ancient wisdom" that guided them.

That wisdom was their Inner Voice. And it's the same wisdom upon which you are now drawing at the root of your being. Each of you are ready to reconnect with this wisdom so that you can live with and from this part of your deeper self.

Living with and from your Inner Voice will guide you to make daily decisions that fit the present moment. You will discover purity in your process, trusting that you will receive a direction from within to find your way forward, no matter what the chaos of any present situation.

You will become your own person, relying solely upon your inner dialog for the answers you seek. You need no longer look outside of yourself for the answers.

As children, our innocence is strongly rooted in this wisdom. We are born with an immediate connection to the inner self that most of us, unfortunately, lose as we grow into adulthood. As kids, we acted out scenarios from within…without being conscious of what was going on around us.

We seemed to live in different worlds and dimensions right next to our parents on any given afternoon in the living room. Maybe it was jumping around fighting an imaginary dragon. Perhaps it was belting out tunes in some fantasy world. Regardless, we were connected to our inner source and lived exclusively in freedom and creativity.

A friend recently told me that she was driving with her five-year-old daughter and out of the blue the little girl said, "Mommy, do you know that dying can be a really good thing?"

My friend found out later that day that her father had passed suddenly from a massive stroke four states away about the same time her daughter made this statement. I see this as the little girl's connection to her grandfather and as an energetic connection to the ancient wisdom that ties us together.

Imagine the child you have seen in its stroller, actively focused on some inner self that has it singing or having a conversation in an imaginary place. This is the place inside of our current adult self that we rediscover as we tap into our Inner Voice.

Now don't try to use the excuse that you can't access this place because you won't fit into your old stroller. Remember that you have upgraded to a car that is as fine a place as any to have a conversation with yourself!

This represents a good place to pause and review what's involved in taking the preliminary steps to connect with your Inner Whisper. Remember, this is easy! All you have to do is pay attention, listen, pause, and take note when you feel that tug… that urge…that pulls at your heart and soul. You can almost hear it, so give it a voice of its own. Let it sing and belt out its aria! Then, if it feels right, just follow it and don't question it.

If you find yourself feeling stuck or confused at times ("Is this my true Inner Voice, my thinking mind, my conscience, or my common sense?"), don't worry; that's perfectly normal. Just turn to any of the sections in this book titled "Your Inner Voice at Work" for coaching reminders to recognize and work with your Inner Whisper. It will feel like your best friend and feel right in your gut. You will intuitively come to know it as it comes up from the core of your being.

Accessing your ancient wisdom might just connect you with your life partner, or to that vehicle you keep feeling, or even a winning lottery number. It might put you on the right road at the right time to place someone in front of you so that you can help change a flat tire or call a tow truck for your favorite movie star.

All the while and no matter the circumstance, you will be interacting with them from your Inner Voice in a connected way with inner wisdom, compassion, and true intention.

By the way, the latter example is one I shared with a famous movie star…a situation that was all Inner Voice-directed. Out of that chance meeting came a connection with a well-known movie producer who became one of my best catering clients.

I mentioned earlier that ancient wisdom guided early indigenous people to their food supply. Foraging was an inner-directed choice of safety versus supply: Is the distance too far, or the terrain full of predators?

My predator-versus-supply situation happened when I received a last-minute staffing request from a chef. She needed a waiter to serve a gathering of celebs at Steve Martin's home on Central Park West for a reading of the actor's recent screenplay.

Finding an available server on such last-minute notice posed a problem…until the chef asked me to step in. After all, I lived just a block away.

The scary predator I faced wasn't the saber-toothed tiger of our ancestors. It was ego, my deep-seated resistance to filling in as the waiter for these famous people when I was a caterer with my own business.

The chef was beside herself with fear, so I listened to the Inner Whisper that guided me to bail her out of a jam. Between silently keeping glasses filled and food moving, I helped the chef create her menus for the upcoming week on location.

As the illustrious guests like Meg Ryan were getting ready to leave, a famous Hollywood screenwriter and director inquired who I was and then requested my business card. Nora Ephron became my catering client for over twelve years.

Ancient wisdom aligns within our Inner Voice by pulling us to our supply. Therefore, our most dangerous predator can be our ego because it blocks our connection to the innate wisdom within us.

Acknowledging this predator offers you the opportunity to hold the connection to your ancient wisdom. Especially now, when this connection can provide a strong anchor, helping you to stay present and live a grounded and more balanced life despite the daily chaos that you may otherwise face.

This ancient wisdom to which you were fully connected as a child will add depth and insight to your life and to the relationships with those you love.

Medicine Doll

It was in my uncle's country grocery store near his rural Montana farm that I saw a Black doll in its box sitting high above me on a shelf when I was five or so years of age.

I still recall some fifty-plus years later my immediate connection with the doll at that moment. I can feel the well-worn old hardwood floorboards beneath my feet as I stood there staring up at her. Something deep inside of me was tied to something greater than the physical doll.

Let me be clear. It wasn't long before everyone in the store knew that I was not leaving without that doll. Already a divine force at that tender age, I was ready to do battle with anyone who thought otherwise. What in the heck a Black doll was doing on the shelf of a rural Montana country store in the 1950s was positive proof that higher forces were at work that day.

The doll brought me even closer to my grandmother because I insisted that she make clothes for it. I can still draw up around me like a blanket the warmth of the absolute love I felt spending time with her as she sewed the doll's wardrobe. I realized years later that I would have had no other reason to spend time with her in any other way without this doll linking us together.

It's an energetic connection that I can still feel as I picture her sitting in her favorite sewing room chair. I can hear her laughter as she accepted specific instructions to execute my design vision. I was aware even then that she appreciated who I was as she helped me accomplish my dream. We each enjoyed the connection of experiencing our life forces and our ancient wisdom working together.

I took the doll to my first day of school, much to my parents' chagrin. My mother tried in vain to talk me out of it, but I would have none of that. When I got home, my mother wanted to know how my day had been. I'm not sure if I told her how the kids teased me, but she said that I decided not to bring the doll to school with me the next day.

And we wonder why we lose our innocence and early connection to see the things we can no longer see as adults. Our inner light dims, weakens, or disconnects as we get older and move farther away from the connection to our wisdom linked to our Inner Voice as our innocence gets banged and dented.

Though the doll remained at home, her power and importance in my life remained significant. I should have called her Medicine Doll. Such was her influence on me and on my parents, who shifted into the unconditionally loving and understanding adults that they became in this lifetime.

The doll served as the vessel that helped to activate the ancient wisdom within my folks that they would need as they raised me. Its presence in my life at that time forced them to kick into gear much earlier than perhaps they had planned. I know that my dragging that Black doll around rural Montana was definitely an experience that my parents never saw coming.

My parents had adopted me and my two siblings from different birth families when we were each under a year. Witness the ancient wisdom and the connection to higher assistance that brought each of us into my parents' home by divine plan.

Within a year or so of the doll's appearance in our lives, I remember my father asking me never to lie to him. He told me, "I am willing to go through anything with you." He proved that to me year after year.

I can still feel the ancient wisdom emanating from inside of him as he uttered that unconditionally loving statement that day. Both he and Mom were rare parents. I had more than a few friends wanting to trade in theirs for mine.

Their love and support were rooted in their inner wisdom. It just emanated from them. My father, especially, lived from his Inner Voice, although he would never have called it that or even had a notion about it or thought about how he connected to it. To him, it was just a natural way of being. Oh sure, he went above the neck on occasion, like the time he realized that I had spent half his silver-dollar collection on candy. But it was rare for him to remain in his thinking mind for long.

His memory serves as a reminder that we can connect to our inner ancient wisdom at any time. It's always ready and available. We don't even have to remember it. It can be activated by something every day in our life. We need only hear it when it speaks.

An Inner Wisdom rests within you. It is always ready and available. You need not remember it. Something every day in your life will activate it.

Our inner wisdom is persistent but quiet. It will always whisper, but it will never stop knocking at your door.

Vironika Tugaleva

Your Inner Voice in Action

> *Ancient wisdom is connected at the soul level*
> *and activates our Inner Whisper.*

For me, ancient wisdom continues to reveal that everything is connected and that there are no mistakes or coincidences.

I am aware of the energy of ancient wisdom if something feels like it has my name on it, such as the black doll, special horses, the blue Y Foil, a silver Jaguar, and my train-station-home at the edge of the Rocky Mountains. Each of these had a physicalness that resonated in me at the soul level.

I had terrific adoptive parents who radiated wisdom in the way they lived their life. When they were both gone, it wasn't long before my birth family showed up in my life.

This extraordinary gift offered me a front-row seat to clarify why I was adopted into the Lindberg home.

I was able to see how the Lindbergs' unconditional loving support set the stage to activate me to pursue every interest I had. All these experiences were in place when I became aware of my mission to write a book raising awareness of the importance of our Inner Voice.

Ancient wisdom runs through each of us and provides the centerline of our path, putting the learnings and experiences in place for this lifetime.

I feel the ancient wisdom as the spark in my life force that surfaces along with my inner knowing.

> Can you think of a time you were aware of a connection to ancient wisdom?

Chapter 14

The Clarity of Your Inner Voice

Sometimes that "voiceless voice" sounds so clear that I want to look to the person next to me and say, "Pardon my Inner Voice if it disturbed you." It's that loud and clear! Or that feeling with words around it may be so strong that it catches my attention like police lights flashing without the siren. I just can't deny its powerful clarity when it grabs my attention.

It might be several words that come through me: "Don't buy the green coffee mug," as I pass a store shelf, or "Sign up for a *Time* magazine subscription," as I stand at a magazine rack. I could be walking through the park and hear, "Call so-and-so now! DON'T WAIT until you get home!"

I never know when it will come, so I have learned to act on it as though time is of the essence. Don't put it off! Don't second-guess it!

There is a clear distinction between acting on the pull from below the neck and acting on a thought impulse coming from above the neck, in the form of what I call the "I Needs" and "Connecting the Dots."

The **"I Needs"** pull sounds like this: "I need a house with a bigger deck for that one time a year I invite people over to watch the Fourth of July parade." Or, "I need to buy that horse trailer because it's a great price, in great shape, and I would love to have a horse."

The "I Needs" often have an outlandish justification accompanying them.

Connecting the Dots sounds like this: "IF I get a cheap flight to Rome, AND find a cheap hotel, AND convince a friend to go with me to split the costs, AND get time off from work, AND save the money for the fare, THEN I can go to Rome."

Connecting the Dots involves trying to figure out each step instead of hearing and feeling your Inner Voice directing you in the actions to take. Our thinking mind is very adept at plotting and planning—Connecting the Dots—and in convincing us we need something.

When you find yourself in that place, remember to go below the neck. There you will find the clarity of your inner pull as it guides you forward.

With clarity comes a raised conscious awareness. It's a new way of living that activates and expands your life. It will become clear when your Inner Voice is trying to show you something. As you raise your conscious awareness of the experience that results from acting on your Inner Voice, you will see the benefits of these unexpected levels of clarity and how they can greatly aid your daily life.

Acting on the clarity coming from within, you will replace the old thinking-mind thoughts that had you Connecting the Dots. The inner you, in whom your trust will grow exponentially, will begin to regularly outvote your thinking mind in your daily decision process. This level of inner clarity lets your decision be finished—truly finished—once it has been made. Talk about the freedom to act!

Remember that an important part of this process is that you are continuing to raise your awareness and gain trust in yourself. The material results are not the only objective; awareness is also a benefit and a powerful step forward on your path. The clarity of an action that you took several days, weeks, or years earlier will be more clearly revealed to you down the road. For now, it is important to welcome conscious awareness as part of your clarity as you grow forward in your life.

Tossing the Television

Working on a writing assignment at my desk one evening, I struggled with my desire to also watch the Summer Olympics. They had always been a big deal in our household. When I was in high school, my father and I planned all our farm work around that telecast.

The TV in my New York office was the last of three sets I had previously owned. It sat on a high shelf attached to the wall behind me. Every time I went to look at the screen, I had to turn all the way around from the writing position at my desk.

I heard my Inner Voice loud and clear when it told me that I could not write and watch TV at the same time. My thinking mind immediately justified that. NO, this was the Summer Olympics, and they wouldn't happen for another four years. At that moment, I allowed my thinking mind to override my Inner Voice's direction.

I began to write and swivel, write and swivel. Then the TV needed some adjustments. So, I got up on my step stool and started working on it. This up-and-down process went on for twenty minutes. Now I wasn't getting ANY writing done or enjoying the telecast!

Then somehow, as I stepped down from the ladder after yet another adjustment, I hooked my foot in the cord and pulled the TV, which crashed to the floor. The case broke but the tube kept playing—and STILL needed adjusting—which now was *really* annoying!

In that next moment, I gained clarity and became consciously aware of the message from my Inner Voice. If I wanted to write not just my assignment, but more importantly, the book that I felt emerging, then it was time to let go of the TV.

It was time for me to become an active participant in MY dream instead of an observer of someone else's dream. I got it! Into the trash went the set. It was the last one I have ever owned.

Pushed from inside that day, I shifted to make my writing a priority over watching TV. I shifted deeper into conscious awareness that there was a book bumping around in me. My thinking mind did not know what the book was about or how it was going to happen. However, I trusted the process would reveal itself as the energy from inside pulled me forward… one day at a time… toward what I felt was true.

Your Inner Voice will always make itself heard when it really counts. Beware of the consequences when you try to ignore it.

*Everyone who wills can hear the Inner Voice.
It is within everyone.*

Mahatma Gandhi

Your Inner Voice in Action

Our Inner Whisper brings a robust accountability for developing our talents and gifts.

Tossing my TV brought an unexpected Inner Voice-directed shift. It was clear the time had come for me to cut down on distractions and make my writing a priority.

Out of the TV's wreckage and removal came a greater insight that I did, indeed, have something within me to say and contribute.

It was glaringly apparent that I had to make tough choices in planning my creative time to act on the book rising within me.

Here are three guidelines that resulted from my TV wreckage:

- Finish working on my creative projects by early afternoon,
- Make it a priority to keep my life as simple as possible to maintain the momentum for my creative projects, and
- Remain vigilant of the amount of time I devote to my creative projects each day, allowing for distractions such as Netflix, socializing, and doing work that isn't creating my desired life.

> What creative accountability is your Inner Voice pulling you to act on?

Chapter 15

A Personal Journey with Your Inner Voice

Living from the inside out is about our personal journey as we honor the pull of our Inner Voice. It is no longer about the Monday-through-Friday work routine. There is a freshness to each day replacing the staleness that otherwise sets in when our thinking mind runs the show. Our inner wisdom encourages us to stretch ourselves in different and unexpected ways in both work and play.

Change is a constant in life whether we like it or not. As we come to accept this universal law, we honor the awareness that we have an Inner Voice to guide us toward greater freedom. As we become more consciously aware, we awaken to a whole new world in front of us.

We can let go of the greatest lies our thinking mind tells us… that security exists outside of ourselves and is achieved by maintaining the status quo. Rather, the truth is that we have free reign in all areas of our lives when we start working from the inside out. Our Inner Voice is all the security we need to embrace the universal Law of Change.

So, let's agree to stop resisting everything that our thinking mind tells us we aren't ready to embrace or can't understand or can't afford.

Say this out loud:

"I commit to stop living a life led by resistance in every decision, opportunity, or daily task. I embrace a new life led by my Inner Voice that I trust completely and in which I will find all the security I need to manifest all that is true for me in this new awareness."

Welcome to the new life flow in your personal journey! You have made the commitment to quit leading with resistance.

So now, things will start to happen. For some wonderful divine reason, the inner you will start to feel the energy of "the sky is the limit." Your personal journey has begun, led by your Inner Voice. Congratulations, this may be the biggest fork in the road decision of your life to date!

Once I actively embraced my Inner Voice, one of the first major shifts I noticed was truly becoming a "people person," a concept that up, until that moment, I had never considered. I was guided to all kinds of people who I would otherwise never have met or considered spending time with. My life opened up exponentially because of it.

I have also become consciously aware that my Inner Voice is guiding me toward the people with whom I am now ready to interact and toward the situations that are specific to my life path. I'm always moved when I reflect on the experiences in which my Inner Voice placed me well before I became consciously aware that I was activated to participate in them.

Within this life flow, I have found the power and joy of my personal journey.

Luncheon with Dr. Mannion

During one of my above-the-neck moments, I decided to transfer schools and major in pre-med, in large part because there was money to be made in it. I enrolled in a private Catholic college because it was noted for placing a high percentage of graduates in medical school. I was an older, non-Catholic student when I transferred in.

As the department head, Dr. Mannion was intimidating both in manner and position to almost everyone in the school. He expected students to remain focused and committed. Serious and stern, his piercing eyes held students in their grip. Everyone felt tense whenever they had to go to his office and discuss something. The collective fear that came up when he asked a question in class was palpable.

I sat in the front of his class where I felt pulled to be by my Inner Voice. It wasn't so that I could answer questions like all the eager smart kids sitting around me. Curiously, about a month into the class, I realized that I was not afraid of Dr. Mannion.

After several months, I visited his office to inquire about some test results. During our brief exchange, I suddenly felt my Inner Voice push me to ask him to join me for lunch.

My thinking mind snapped to full alert as it heard the invitation pass over my lips. I remember the knot in my stomach and feeling lightheaded as the oxygen supply was cut off to my brain. My thinking mind yelled that this was a terrible idea!

As I stood in front of his desk, my thinking mind perceived that Dr. Mannion was trying to make sure that he had heard me clearly, in preparation to bite off my head. But, as he sat there staring at me, I noticed the curl of a smile forming on his lips.

"No one has ever had the guts to ask me to lunch," he said. "They are all too afraid of me. Yes, I'd like to go to lunch with you, Erec."

My thinking mind silently expressed my gratitude–and relief.

And so it was that Dr. Mannion and I began having lunch every month. We talked and laughed about many things. As I mentioned in an earlier personal story that acting from your Inner Voice will catch the attention of other people, word spread like a brushfire that Dr. Mannion and I were lunching. What did it all mean?

By then, I wasn't concerned about these outer appearances because my Inner Voice did most of the talking during those lunches. It asked him all the questions I had inside—the ones I would have never had the opportunity to ask in an office or classroom setting. Out of these questions came an inner clarity for my life path.

During our third lunch, I became aware that I was finished with the pre-med program and wanted to own a restaurant instead. Dr. Mannion respected and supported my decision. Through our time together, I would come to better understand that something inside was pulling me in another direction that my thinking mind had never considered.

My Inner Voice deserves full credit for this opportunity to expand. My thinking mind was a chicken sh-t and would NEVER have allowed me this sharp turn in the road. My lunches with Dr. Mannion became pivotal for receiving the necessary information to take my next turn in the road and buy a business instead of continuing pre-med classes. I'm grateful for my Inner Voice coming through me with that luncheon invitation, even if it did shake the structure of my physical and mental being.

◇◇◇◇◇◇◇◇◇◇◇◇◇◇◇◇◇◇◇◇◇◇◇◇◇◇◇◇◇◇◇◇◇◇◇◇◇◇

> As you step into your personal journey and
> trust your inner guidance, you will experience
> a clearer vision as you proceed forward.
> The people and places will be supplied.

◇◇◇◇◇◇◇◇◇◇◇◇◇◇◇◇◇◇◇◇◇◇◇◇◇◇◇◇◇◇◇◇◇◇◇◇◇◇

Practice listening to your intuition, your Inner Voice; ask questions; be curious, see what you hear; and then act upon what you know to be true. These intuitive powers were given to your soul at birth.

Clarissa Pinkola Estes

Your Inner Voice in Action

*A staircase facilitates inner-directed career clarity
with each new level.*

The lunch invitation was groundbreaking. It gave me first-hand experience that my Inner Voice's guidance would flow right out my mouth to redirect my life.

By the third lunch with Dr. Mannion, I could feel shifts resulting from conversations directed by my Inner Voice. Questions I didn't know I had continued to rise through me, and I had the perfect person to answer them. It was all thanks to my Inner Voice arranging these lunches.

Our lunches resulted in an unexpected outcome, bringing another fork in my life path, similar to being guided to quit my classes to ski. So, yet again, the Inner Whisper guided me forward with my life path.

I walked away from my interaction with Dr. Mannion with expanded inner confidence because of the career redirection.

I saw how these lunches boosted my momentum for approaching my dad to back me in a restaurant.

Acting on our Inner Voice is like a staircase. The inner direction leads to raising consciousness, which then shows us our next expanded step until we reach the top.

> What inner message aren't you letting escape your lips?
> It could be invaluable in showing you the way forward.

Chapter 16

Growing into the Energy of Your Inner Voice

As you raise your awareness by hearing, trusting, and acting on your Inner Voice, you will feel the energy flow up within you as it continues to grow more powerful. What begins as a mere pulse will develop into a strong, steady push. This is where the fun REALLY begins! The increased energy flow will help you expand into areas of yourself that you have not used or remain unaware of.

The growth in your Inner Voice flow is two-fold: you step into your Self, and you step into your Life.

Suddenly, it feels like you can experience life as you have always wanted. Current opportunities expand, and new opportunities present themselves in proportion to the increased energy coming through you.

Your Inner Voice will activate new areas of energy flow as it pushes you to face your truths. These flows could include expansion in your career or, perhaps, the realization that it is no longer fulfilling. This additional energy might also reactivate the nine-year-old artist in you. It might push you to write, take singing lessons, rent a cabin for the summer, join a seaside timeshare, enroll in Toastmasters, or ask your divorced neighbor out on a date.

You may have never considered these scenarios, but the energy coming through your Inner Voice is now making you aware of a strong pull to dive into them. Let's remember that the stretch is about expanding beyond familiar and comfortable things. It is about (re)discovering those parts of you that have remained hidden or buried, perhaps for years.

Avoid the pitfall of going above the neck into your thinking mind to analyze why you suddenly want to take a yoga class, write a blog, or work in an upscale jewelry store as a second job. Maybe you have always been a gemologist inside, but you weren't aware of this until your Inner Voice energy activated you.

Take a moment to consider whether your current life is filled with distractions…or how you feel on Sunday evening when you realize that Monday morning is around the corner. Are you happy? Growing into your Inner Voice and honoring your awareness to step into its pull will reveal more of your true self than you ever expected.

Inner Voice-directed growth is never about preparing for what you are being called to experience. You'll just feel the inner energy leading you into an unknown event or situation. Just take the next step; it's about time you let it come out! Allow it to flow from within and up through you and experience its truth about who you are.

The Restaurant

After hearing my Inner Voice at age nineteen, I grew more comfortable living from it. I still wasn't aware enough to understand the difference between a thinking-mind 'thought' and an Inner-Voice feeling connected to a thought. Consequently, I made a bunch of right-and-left turns on my path forward.

Growing into my Inner Voice energy was two-fold: it took me to the next step within my SELF and the next step in my LIFE. Growth is found in both our personal unfolding and life experiences.

When I left the pre-med program in college, I felt certain about opening a restaurant. I could feel the pull of a business coming up from within as more of the entrepreneur started to surface.

Unbeknownst to me, my thinking mind was still very much a part of the decision-making process, although I was not yet consciously aware enough to realize it. It held the belief that I could live happily-ever-after by owning a Mexican restaurant in a beautiful mountain town, tied to the pulse of the local university, and with a ski hill close enough that I could work through lunch and ski every afternoon. Sounds pretty good to the thinking mind, right?

After six years of owning the restaurant and experiencing that lifestyle, I had received plenty of growth both in self and in life… only the self was completely bored and consequently unhappy with the life that it had created.

The entrepreneur in me had succeeded, but it had also saddled me with payroll, seven-day workweeks, and manning the kitchen when an employee didn't show. I learned that owning a business took its pound of flesh even while it was lucrative and despite the fun at times.

Why did I ever let myself think that making tacos for the rest of my life was the pinnacle of who I am or what I came here to do? That's scary as I look back now!

My thinking mind had settled for security and lifestyle over progressive inner growth and truthful living. Sure, there was a picturesque mountain town with lots of distractions and the added security of being my own boss. Yet, I worked more long days than I wanted to admit. More importantly, I was sacrificing my inner expansion and creative expression.

In fact, my Inner Voice pushed so strongly against this lifestyle that I felt, at times, like I was dying inside.

Outside of work, I pursued drinking and other distractions to avoid the truth. I was very unhappy, and I could feel my Inner Voice pulling me to New York City.

Our thinking mind will NEVER create the life we truly want.

*Following your inner guidance
has a unique power all its own.
Even when others can't understand it,
you can feel your soul being pulled
to the place it truly belongs.*

Kianu Starr

Your Inner Voice in Action

Our Inner Whisper provides a significant auto-correct when we set the bar too low.

From a soul perspective, owning a restaurant awakened the entrepreneur in me. It proved invaluable to have this quality activated in my mid-twenties and became the foundational springboard for my future. The experience gave me the strength, boldness, and insight for the long haul in creating my Inner-Voice directed projects.

I didn't realize the restaurant lifestyle was a trap, in that I had set the bar too low for the inner me. The daily routine did not stimulate my Inner-Voice's connection to what I came to do in this lifetime.

With the entrepreneur activated, it would still take years of personal learning and life experience before I reached a career height that fulfilled me. Writing books, coaching, and speaking on the Inner Voice's importance didn't reveal itself until my fifties.

Sharing these stories with others would be instrumental in raising awareness of the power and importance of the Inner Voice…what I really came here to do!

> Looking back, can you see times where you have set the bar too low?

Chapter 17

Your Inner Voice and the Fork in the Road

YOU WILL FIND FREEDOM when you live in the flow of your Inner Voice. It is the foundation on which you can rely as you face the fork in the road of life's daily challenges and decisions on the way to becoming who you are.

With every Inner Voice-directed choice you make, you gain the strength to face these future forks in your life path with enthusiasm and confidence. This will help you replace the angst and worry that result when making decisions from the thinking mind. Be aware that choosing the path to who you are may often lead you away from everything that looked and felt familiar.

In the past, when you lived in your thinking mind, you may have missed these forks completely. Or the forks may have brought such fear of the unknown that you could only choose the path that felt familiar to your thinking mind, rather than the path to who you are.

By working from your Inner Voice, however, you can better understand, accept, and face changes or obstacles because it is connected to passions and attractions coming from that fork. The outer appearances—or the outsized consequences that your thinking mind would otherwise create—simply fall away.

Decisions that your thinking mind once told you had to be made from your comfort zone will now be made from the freedom of true expression powered by your Inner Voice. This guidance will move you forward without allowing the outer appearances to exert any power over your choice.

You have already faced a fork in the road since your Inner Voice led you to read these pages. Pat yourself on the back. You have chosen the path toward finding your true self. Hooray for you!

One of the most powerful results of using your Inner Voice to make decisions at these life junctures is that you will begin to feel the need to let go of things that no longer serve or fulfill you. You will consciously embrace this shift in activities, people, and possessions that will come into your life or drop away.

A Fork in the Road

Once I came to the deeper realization that I felt empty and hollow, despite the lifestyle that my restaurant brought me, my thinking mind finally gave way and allowed my Inner Voice to kick into action. Holding myself accountable to Inner-Voice direction meant staying below the neck and out of the strong current of the outer appearances as I faced my reality. My Inner Voice was pulling me toward New York City and a career singing jingles for TV and radio commercials. Talk about a fork in the road!

It directed me to list the restaurant for sale. Four interested buyers immediately approached me. I had six years remaining on the lease, but every buyer wanted an additional four years added to it to create a ten-year lease (a standard practice in the area). The lawyer who represented the landlord came back with the news that the landlord wanted an additional and ludicrous $30,000 annual rent to extend the lease. The buyers disappeared.

Shortly after delivering the bad news, the lawyer pondered. "I don't know what my client's thinking," he said, "because you could easily file bankruptcy and break the lease."

My thinking mind went into spasms. What? Bankruptcy? After running a successful restaurant for the past six years? I would need all the money from the sale to support my lifestyle when I move to New York City.

My Inner Voice, meanwhile, pushed me to talk to my dad who would be left holding the bag as the financial backer. My thinking mind screamed, "Oh no, not a good idea...he will be furious!" As I drove the long distance to my parents' home, my thinking mind kicked into overdrive as it considered every possible scenario to justify my actions.

Arriving home, I finally got below my neck and my Inner Voice presented my position to my dad. I told him:

"I feel pulled to sell the restaurant and move to New York City; the interested buyers have disappeared due to the landlord's demands to change the lease; the lawyer said I could file bankruptcy and break the lease. Since you put up cash and stocks to finance my restaurant, you will lose your money."

While yelling was never a common occurrence in our household, the ensuing heated exchange between us definitely presented a new fork in THAT road! As my Inner Voice continued to stand its ground with my dad, my mother watched wide-eyed and silent as the drama unfolded.

Yet it was all over in less than ten minutes. My dad paused, momentarily collecting his thoughts, and then said, "I don't like losing money, but I don't want you to stay in something that you don't want to do. I want to watch you live your life. Consider this money to be part of your inheritance. We can sell the land and use our assets in the areas that you kids are interested in expressing yourselves."

As he spoke, I could hear my dad's Inner Voice and feel the power emanating from within him. At that moment, his unconditional love for me reinforced the lesson. Following my Inner Voice was the ONLY way I would ever live from this moment forward.

Life renews itself at each fork in the road when we act from our Inner Voice.

The best vision is insight.

Malcolm Forbes

Your Inner Voice in Action

> *Obstacles fall away when we speak our truth*
> *in unconditional love.*

Look at the outer appearances in confronting my father. I not only had to face a heated situation suggesting bankruptcy and the loss of his money, but I also needed to enlist his financial support to move to New York. I was in stratospheric overwhelm on the 180-mile drive home.

It was life-changing for me to hear my father's Inner Voice state, "I don't want you to stay in something you don't want to do. I want to watch you live your life."

I continue to embrace these two enlightening sentences as ancient wisdom passed down from a father to his son, which continues to be a cornerstone for all my decisions.

I felt a powerful, loving, unconditional support, on a cellular level, the minute he expressed it. As always, he stood dead center of who he was and didn't back down from the situation at hand. I knew in that decisive moment that life didn't get any better than this!

Your Inner Voice will pull you to stand in unconditionally loving support no matter how difficult the circumstances.

Following my father's conversation, my thinking mind and ego had to face steep disappointment around my expectations of going to New York with plenty of money from my business sale. This financial setback was very hard for my thinking mind's expectations, but I could also feel exhilaration, directing me forward to the Big Apple.

My father's unconditional loving answer is a powerful example of how perceived obstacles fall away when we stay in our truth and speak from our Inner Voice.

Never believe you are trapped when living from the guidance of your Inner Voice.

> Can you think of a situation when you spoke with unconditional love in speaking your truth?

Chapter 18

Your Inner Voice and the Trailblazer in You

Living from your Inner Voice will soon turn you into a trailblazer with a new zest for life!

Taking that fork in the road leads you boldly into the unknown, leaving behind a path fraught with boredom, unconsciousness, and unfulfilling mediocrity. As a trailblazer, you sit in the pilot's seat, checking out the runway as you take off toward an open horizon. You will recognize your flight path by the energetic inner pull that leads you forward.

As a trailblazer, you may not know what to do next or in which direction to head, but you won't have to know the answer ahead of time. Because you are living from the inner knowing that guides you every step of the way, you will feel the answer lies in you and trust the trailblazer in you (your Inner Voice) to pull you forward. No longer will you feel the need to (or will you attempt to) control the unknowns through your thinking mind.

I want to encourage the trailblazer in you to trust yourself with daily decisions in ways that you never have. My intention as your coach is to be here for you as you connect with your inner power. Let me show you how this works.

No one has power over the trailblazer in you because the trailblazer is YOU, activated from inside. As a trailblazer, you no longer need someone to save you, pay your way, or help you survive. You don't need the approval of others, nor do you need to look outside of yourself for someone to give you the answers. Or give you the money you think you need. Or give you the love that you seek. The answers are no longer outside of you.

Trailblazers are teachers whose lives reflect their message. They set examples to friends, family, and coworkers who see them living in ways that they are too afraid to attempt. They will wonder how you can do it, and they may wonder how you suddenly had these ideas and the confidence to act on them.

Trailblazers are inventors and entrepreneurs. Working from their Inner Voices as they faced the unknowns in their lives, the trailblazers before us created the conveniences we enjoy today.

Like them, all you need to do is simply activate your bravery software by trusting in your inner knowing. Recognize that it is not about the outer appearances—or HOW to do it. Rather, it's about being aware that the answer has always been lying right there inside of you all the time.

Trailblazers simply choose not to follow the rules created by man. Rather, they remain attuned to and follow the rules of earth and nature as they break new ground for the rest to follow. Consider that it may just be YOUR time to lead others using the gifts that you brought into this lifetime to share…. gifts that reflect who you are and what you came here to do.

Roping Lessons

The trailblazer in me awakened that morning on the sidewalk when I heard my Inner Voice for the first time. I ditched my class and headed back to the dorm to flop down on my bed and reflect on the morning's events. My thinking mind was scared, numb, and resistant now that I had connected to this new power within me.

My Inner Voice illuminated the truth of what I was feeling inside… that this decision to stop attending my classes and ski was a critical juncture in my life. It wasn't about trying to understand why no one else around me was on this path. I lay on my bed most of the day, rising long enough to eat a quick lunch and dinner. Finally, I went to sleep.

I awoke the next morning and headed for breakfast without a clue as to what my actions would be that day. After breakfast, I walked back to my room and felt the pull from inside to put on my ski clothes. My thinking mind immediately started screaming, "No don't do it! You are really going to get it from your father!" Yet I dressed, grabbed my skis, and headed to my car.

As I drove off campus, I was acutely aware that all the traffic was coming toward me as students arrived for morning classes. I was the only one going in the opposite direction as I headed toward the ski hill.

For the entire school quarter, I became the trailblazer on my dorm floor. My chosen path of skiing all day long every day activated the other students. (Just as you will activate the people in your life as you allow your inner trailblazer to come forth!) My peers would be feeling the pressure of an upcoming test or a late assignment, and I would appear worn out from a hard day of skiing moguls.

A second powerful experience that quarter affirmed that I must continue to do what felt right to me. Once a week, I would give a roping lesson (I had been schooled by a world champion) to another ranch kid on my floor. He was always so serious and rigid about following the rules, and he constantly worried about his studies.

It was only at these weekly roping sessions where I saw him laugh and be playful. It appeared he was living his passion during our nickel-betting competitions. The following summer he was cleaning a gun and it somehow went off and killed him. This sad event made me grateful that I had offered him an opportunity to laugh and enjoy a different aspect of his college experience.

His short life reaffirmed that I must continue to trust and act on my Inner Voice above all else.

It made me even more thankful that I had honored my Inner Voice's direction. Spending that winter alone, pushed from inside to ski the slopes, changed the course of my life. It continues to influence how I make a choice or decision today. My Inner Voice opened the door for me to become who I am in this lifetime.

Connecting with the trailblazer within you is a critical juncture that will open up your life in ways you've never imagined. The benefits are boundless for you, and they will activate the people you care about.

We open inner and outer doors when we honor the trailblazer in ourselves.

Knowing many things doesn't teach insight.

Herodotus

Your Inner Voice in Action

> *Our Inner Voice is the doorway*
> *into the last frontier within each of us.*

I chose "trailblazer" because the inner me was now leading the thinking me into some unimagined territory. There was no one but me to lead after quitting my classes to ski. At some point each day, I would continue to feel the rightness of the pull from inside.

Our Inner Voice is the access to the last frontier for each of us. It is ready to be mined, as valuable as California's goldfields during the Gold Rush, and we don't have any travel expenses to reach it.

Looking back, I see this college semester as the most significant preparation for my future, a crucial fork into the whisper within me, and the most valuable quarter of my years of classes.

That winter on the ski hill taught me to own my life preparation. The decision to ski also allowed me to increase my communication skills with people as I dealt with their confusion about quitting my classes.

It soon became apparent that I would no longer be someone who followed society's herd mentality once I chose to honor the pull of my Inner Voice.

Watching the ranch kid putting excessive pressure on himself about grades and following his dad's expectations, instead of exploring his interests, left me with feelings of discomfort and sadness.

Looking back, I view his college experience and death as part of a soul contract he chose for this lifetime. I hold this same soul contract belief that I chose my cancer as part of my learning in this lifetime.

> Are you aware of any part of the last frontier within you that your Inner Voice is pulling you to prospect?
>
> What soul contract do you feel you chose?

Chapter 19

Your Inner Voice and Your Highest Visions

Our highest visions are those dreams and desires that originate from our Inner Voice and represent the truest parts of who we are. Our dreams and desires become those visions that we can feel and see in our mind's eye. They just feel "right" to us.

There have been times on my life's path where my highest visions have not been at the forefront of my focused efforts. Rather, my efforts were goal-directed. I now realize that these goals originated from my thinking mind as I attempted to connect the dots toward their achievement.

Dreams and desires that lay deeper within me would pop up at times out of nowhere, but my thinking mind would discount them as unbelievable and too amazing to be real. Or it would immediately go to the "how to's" or "how could's" and then delete my dreams and desires from my awareness.

However, with my thinking-mind detours behind me, I find that my highest visions remain safely anchored. They merely awaited my rediscovery once I released my thinking mind's perceived "failures" that had overpowered and suppressed these dreams and desires.

Once I wholeheartedly heard, trusted, and acted on my Inner Voice's guidance, I better understood the distinction that my goals were mentally fabricated, whereas my Highest Visions flowed naturally as an authentic feeling within me. The latter carries a distinct energy that I intuitively "know"—IF I stay below the neck and allow my Inner Voice to lead the way.

For example, my initial attempts to write a book felt too emotionally overwhelming for my thinking mind to consider emanating from my highest vision. In paralyzing fear, I would approach writing from above the neck and my thinking mind, thereby lowering the frequency of my highest vision to that of a mere "goal"—one accompanied by thinking-mind doubts that I could ever write a book. I became stuck in my role as a "doer-thinker."

Goals carry lower-vibrational energy because they originate from a thinking mind conditioned to believe that we must sweat and sacrifice to achieve them. Mere goals don't allow our inner pull to carry us forward easily. The inner pull becomes too big for the analytical brain to process without becoming overwhelmed. The thinking mind lowers the frequency of the energy to accept it at a level it can comfortably process based upon its belief-system conditioning.

So, even as the energy of my highest vision pulled me forward to write a book, my thinking mind created doubt energy that conflicted with the inner pull, thereby dragging it down. I was left to roll around in confusion that came hand in hand with thinking…that is, until I chose to completely drop below the neck. Only then could I fully hear, trust, and act on my Inner Voice to honor that highest vision to write *Your Brilliant Inner Whisper*.

Let's pause here to give you some further examples that distinguish the highest visions from mere analytical goals so you can see how they differ. Remember, your highest visions will feel vast, and their energetic pull will direct you to create a fulfilling life. These include:

- Owning the feeling that my book is not only real but published and an international bestseller. My intention is to shift global consciousness forward.

- Connecting to my inner knowing and using those spiritual tools that resonate with me to create freedom in whatever areas (including personal expression) I feel pulled to create.

- Creating a world talk that will expand people's awareness to see who they are and what they came here to do.

- Opening my heart enough so that I am the first one to reach out my hand to greet a friend or (perceived) enemy in equal measure.

- Demonstrating to the world that it need not be true (nor ever has been) that the older we get, the more we let our highest visions slip away.

- Demonstrating to the world that we can attain our highest visions as we grow older instead of simply "retiring" and letting them slip away.

All of us have, at some time, ignored our Inner Voice as it spoke to us from the place where our highest visions live. Instead, we remained in our thinking mind where doubt lives, and where we shut out or downgraded our highest visions to mere goals. In doing so, we only added the sweat, and sacrifice, and suffering we (falsely) believed was necessary to achieve them.

Would Dad Have Done It Differently?

Much of my life has been spent in the pursuit of my highest visions and being led by my Inner Voice. However, it was not until I fully understood that I must remain below the neck and out of my thinking mind that I began to appreciate the ease of accomplishing those visions without the worry or doubt that ensued when I tried to connect the dots.

I was lucky that my adoptive parents, and especially my dad, allowed me the opportunity to always keep a toehold on my soul's highest visions.

While out hauling hay one day with my dad, my Inner Voice suddenly asked him, "Would you do anything in your life differently if given the chance?"

He fell surprisingly silent, unusual for him since he was smart, insightful, and always verbally available. We headed back out to the field for another load of hay without any response to my question.

I always marveled at how my father's life fit him like a kid glove. He maintained his own pace with work and play, a steady rhythm by which he lived. He always found the time to stop back by the house for a midmorning coffee or a couple hands of cards with friends who may have come by. He managed to avoid distraction, enjoy the process of his life, and still accomplish everything with ease.

For years, my thinking mind pondered whether I could find a career that fit me with the same joy and freedom that he shared with farming. Notice that part of my process was using my thinking mind to observe my father and try to connect the dots, while my Inner Voice felt the truth in the way he conducted his everyday life.

As we returned from the field and began unloading the truck, he finally answered my earlier question. His "initial" response was that he should have taken the bigger farm that his dad wanted him to have.

He and my mom met and married in California during the war. When it ended, they returned to Montana where he already owned land. When his dad offered to help him buy a larger place, he and mom talked it over and decided they didn't want all the responsibility that came with it. My grandfather's ranch required numerous full-time hired men, and Dad knew deep within himself that he did not want the daily burden of directing workers.

Still, in his life-review process, he told me that my question caused him to reflect on that earlier decision to turn down the offer of a larger farm and the additional income it would have provided. While he had always supported every one of our interests, considering that I was the most "expensive" of the three children triggered him to suddenly question if he should have done his life differently for all of us.

And then he looked me in the eye and said, "I wouldn't do my life any differently."

At that moment, I knew inside that I, too, wanted to speak that truth at the end of my life.

Back then, I lacked the awareness that my father was deeply rooted in his Inner Voice, that place deep inside from which he made all of his decisions. Nevertheless, I could feel by how he spoke and lived day-to-day that it was the place from which I also wanted to live my life.

However, in my youth, I set my goals in my thinking mind. So, I tried to connect the dots to duplicate what I could feel he had in his life, rather than allowing my Inner Voice to guide me toward my highest visions.

Writing *Your Brilliant Inner Whisper* and reflecting on the freedom that I needed to experience every personal story is proof that I can reach the end of my life and say with heartfelt joy, "I wouldn't do it differently."

> *Remain aware of the vastness that you feel in your highest visions. This is where your truth lives and awaits you to step forward into it.*

*When we hear our Inner Voice and follow it,
we can walk our own path.*

Ilchi Lee

Your Inner Voice in Action

> *Being able to say you wouldn't do it differently is a life-changing platform to live by.*

My dad's clarity that he would not do his life differently had a profound effect on me. It was a decisive moment in my awakening and a foundational piece in who I was to become.

It activated me on a cellular level, freed me by creating a life goal to shoot for, and motivated me to believe that it was attainable.

I also felt an inner knowing to trust myself in a way I didn't mentally understand at eighteen. This powerful imprint was now in place for the rest of my life.

There were many times during my youth when I asked myself how I could find a career that fit me, as farming fulfilled my father. I didn't know then that the real question should have been how I could connect with my Inner Voice as my father had.

For much of my life path, I didn't understand that it's not what you do for work; it's about acting on the pull of your Inner Voice to step into what you came here to be.

Today I see that the strength to follow through with my inner knowing to quit my classes to ski had direct roots back to the "I would not do it differently" conversation with my dad.

Are you ready to say from today forward, "I would not do my life differently?"

If yes, what action comes with this committed awareness?

Chapter 20

Raising Your Frequency through Your Inner Voice

I want to salute you for your efforts thus far as you learn to connect with your Inner Voice. Consider this next chapter to be an energetic marker in your progress. The content we are exploring that includes the Law of Manifestation will further impact all of your future decisions in many profound ways.

As you learn to recognize and hold the higher energetic frequency tied to your highest visions, becoming consciously aware as you connect to and act on your Inner Voice's direction, you will manifest those highest visions into reality.

Just as you choose the frequencies of your favorite radio stations, your Inner Voice chooses the frequencies matching those of your highest visions.

As you hear, trust, and act on your Inner Voice's direction, you become more consciously aware of everything that surrounds you. Maintaining that state of being, in turn, raises your frequency, which helps you to feel your way forward through a heightened perception of all areas in your daily life.

Soon you will attract new people and experiences into your life. At the same time, you will let go of activities, job or career interests, friends, and behaviors that no longer serve you. In time, these choices will be replaced by others that fit better with your higher frequency.

As I elevate and maintain a higher frequency each day, I bring positive and lasting change to all aspects of my life. I experience more opportunities to enjoy quality free time, to create emotionally supportive friendships, enjoy a broader range of stimulating conversations, experience daily laughter, and most importantly, validate that I have manifested my dreams into reality.

Even my living space becomes charged with this elevated frequency. For a while, my Montana home became a gathering place or an energetic salon. It was clear that those who walked in the door were directly tied to the frequency I was holding at that moment in time.

Raising my frequency has brought a significant increase in clarity. Any areas of my life that I need to release and that are not an energetic fit become readily apparent. Like a domino effect, as I let go of my attachment to frequencies tied to choices that do not reflect my highest visions, other frequencies tied to new interests and ways of expression show up to replace them. These choices will lead me closer to who I am and what I came here to do.

Shifting to a higher frequency has influenced how I earn my income based on the effort I put into it. I work less but earn more. My abundance has been consistently supplied in much easier and more straightforward ways. The key is to maintain that connection between elevated frequency and Inner Voice-directed actions through complete trust in what I am directed to do each moment.

So, what does elevated frequency mean for you? Let's use an example of a dream or desire that you may have, such as a trip to Rome, Italy. This dream trip holds an energetic frequency for you. It's an exciting international adventure of a lifetime. If it's a new car that you desire, so be it. But know that this dream has a different frequency than the Rome trip.

All aspects of your life—conditions, situations, choices, decisions, and actions—carry a unique frequency attached to them. Consider the frequency involved in the chore of mowing that huge backyard, in one-hundred-degree heat, on your only day off in the last three weeks. It vibrates a lower frequency than the higher frequencies of a trip to Rome or a new car more directly tied to your dreams and desires.

Consider that your highest frequency is directly related to your greatest passion in this particular moment. The chore holds a lower frequency than the dream or desire of a trip to Rome. The longer you can hold onto that feeling of passion or bliss tied to your dream or desire, the longer you remain at that higher frequency.

You must prioritize your focus in other areas tied to lower frequencies to hold several higher frequencies in place.

Your Inner Voice serves you well as your guide. In fact, it is the ONLY way that you will be able to hold those higher frequencies that match those of your dreams and desires. Your Inner Voice will often prioritize the frequencies of situations, choices, decisions, and actions in ways that your thinking mind never could.

If you rely only on your thinking mind to prioritize your actions tied to achieving your dreams and desires, you will never achieve or maintain those matching frequencies. Going above the neck simply disconnects you from, or significantly reduces the level of, those higher frequencies because you are inundated by distractions related to outer appearances.

None of us were taught that to manifest our dreams and desires, we must match and hold the frequencies tied to them by remaining consciously aware of their direct connection to our Inner Voice. The Inner Voice is the only tool powerful enough to hold those higher frequencies once we are aware of their truth.

Consistently acting at lower-level frequencies (distractions and chores), rather than holding the frequencies of our dreams and desires in highest priority is why many of us are so good at maintaining the former and not achieving the latter. It just seems easier to remain in the lower frequency levels no matter how difficult the realities of those circumstances may be.

It is why we work in jobs or pursue careers that don't fit, remain in stale relationships, and live paycheck to paycheck instead of creating conditions that reflect abundance tied to the higher frequencies that are a truer fit for us.

When we experience an insight that feels true—like a trip to Rome, a new car, or writing a book—we must remain consciously aware of the specific frequency that connects to and matches each of these dreams or desires. This is where our Inner Voice becomes invaluable. One of its specialties is to feel an awareness of, and connection to, the specific frequencies tied to our dreams and desires. In each moment, it will lead us to our choices, decisions, and actions that are directly tied to reaching these highest visions.

You're probably wondering how to tie this all together. My next story will show you a good example of this process, which is really quite simple.

First, all you need to do is maintain a conscious awareness of when, where, and how your Inner Voice is directing you to act and then follow its lead. It is an opportunity that, unfortunately, most of us don't take. Instead, we remain above the neck, focusing on the when, where, or how you can get to Rome. This latter path will never work out or get you on the plane.

Here's how you do it.

Become aware of the frequency of what you want to manifest, something that rings true for you or deeply resonates with your higher self. What is the *essence* of your desire? What higher state of being does it represent to you—freedom, joy, excitement, stability, expansion, or self-expression? Visualize and feel yourself aligning with that essence of your dream or desire AND with your Inner Voice.

Remember that YOU must match the frequency, or feeling essence, of your dreams and desires to manifest them into reality.

The Frequency of Being Cool

One evening, as I shared dinner with some friends in my Montana home, a guest turned to me and said, "You were probably always cool. Some people are just born that way."

My initial response, intending to be funny, was to turn around and look behind me to see if he was talking to someone else. He had no idea how far from that truth I was in my earlier years, especially when I remained stuck above the neck in my thinking mind.

I was surprised at his implication that I had somehow always been "cool." This was a man whose portfolio of homes, properties, and hedge funds, by material standards, would be considered way cooler than me.

I realized his statement reflected his thinking mind's need to label its perception of my higher frequency as we interacted through dinner. As I had become more consciously aware, thereby raising my frequency, I had become accustomed to how others, like him, perceived me. (You can expect comments about how healthy, young, vibrant, and calm you appear to those around you. And well, yes, cool. You will find complete strangers drawn to you who "want what you're enjoying," energetically speaking.)

During our dinner conversation, I explained that I was flying once a month from New York into Montana to host a friend who performed energetic healings on people in a barn studio down the hill from my house. I told him how amazing it was to have a waiting list of people wanting sessions on a windy, remote hillside in the middle of nowhere.

Upon hearing this, he immediately responded, "I want to do that! I want one of those sessions." His wife, sitting beside him, exclaimed in utter disbelief, "You've never even had a massage!" He retorted, "I don't care, I want one!" She then quickly followed up with, "Well, if you're having one, then I am too!"

As I watched their exchange, another friend held up her hand and mouthed silently, "Me too!"

The frequency of who you are radiates out from you and activates everyone and everything around you.

*Hard work leads to low returns.
Insight and doing what we want
leads to high returns.*

Richard Koch

Your Inner Voice in Action

Inner Voice-directed living may look to others like you have customized your life to fit you.

My friend's reference to me "as probably always being cool" reflects his perception of my results from living an Inner-Voice directed life.

I would describe his cool label as the honesty in allowing the flow of my self-expression.

Setting up a once-a-month healing weekend was Inner-Voice directed and generated an immediate waiting list of people lining up for sessions.

These weekends started after I was nudged to pay for a remote healing for a neighboring rancher who was badly hurt when his vehicle overturned. I didn't know him well, so I had no idea how he would take this kind of offer. But my Inner Voice kept prompting me to make the phone call.

Upon hearing my offer of a remote session, he shared that his grandmother had been involved in Native American ceremonies and that she had witnessed actual levitations. So, yes, he was game for this session.

When he received healing results, he asked if he could get another session, but this one in person. I had an insight that my writing studio down the hill in the barn would work great for these sessions since it was a beautiful space with a wood stove to keep it toasty warm.

The healing sessions took off from there, and it was fun to fly from New York to Montana once a month to help people.

This example of trusting the Inner Whisper to call someone I hardly knew to offer remote healing may look cool from the outside, but it's another example of choosing a life of inner-directed self-expression.

> Who are you being nudged to help that you are resisting?

Chapter 21

Your Inner Voice and Reading Higher-Frequency Material

Reading insightful material that further motivates you to live and act from your Inner Voice is one of the best ways to become consciously aware once you start working from inside yourself. This further elevates your frequency as your Inner Voice pulls you forward toward your highest visions.

Ask friends and bookstores for recommendations. I keep a stack of reading material within reach of my office chair. My daily early morning quiet time is spent reading several pages in a book to which my Inner Voice has pulled me. You will be amazed at how fast such reading activates you to drop into your inner self. Over time, you will find that this practice will elevate your personal and professional insights.

Simply select the subject matter that resonates best with you right at that moment where you are on your path. For some this may mean material that builds upon deeply ingrained religious beliefs. Others may be so turned off by negative religious conditioning that any mention of God or spirituality immediately causes paralysis in their thinking minds.

Accordingly, it may be motivational or self-help content whose religious neutrality best serves your needs. Remember that this is *your* life, and you are free to choose your reading material, spiritual beliefs, and the tools for reaching deeper into the core of who you are. You are no longer living by someone else's rules.

Choose topics that activate and expand you forward, rather than choosing the same type of material that merely reinforces concepts with which you already feel comfortable. You will feel and hear your Inner Voice awaken and begin to speak to you. It will have an opinion, inspiration, activation, insight, or forward pull.

In the beginning, some of the books that you choose or that are referred to you may not make any sense. It's okay to put them aside for now and move on to something that stimulates your Inner Voice. There is no coincidence that reading material that expands your awareness will show up in your daily routine. It is part of the process. Stay below the neck, and you will be pulled to the more advanced matter in divine timing.

All reading material has a unique energetic frequency that is tied to its message. As we connect with and absorb the meaning, we raise our frequency to match that frequency. As our frequency is elevated, we are drawn to a wider range of content that serves to further elevate our frequency and bring us deeper into conscious awareness.

In most of my reading material, I highlight those passages to which I most deeply pulled. This holds me accountable for an actual connection with the frequency of the material's message. It also facilitates revisiting those passages to energetically reactivate myself to those frequencies.

Revisiting the highlighted passages to which I feel pulled further enables me to observe which resources brought teachings, beliefs, or awareness that have demonstratively produced results in my life. In turn, those concepts become the tools that I incorporate into my daily practice to maintain and expand my life below the neck.

I purchase most of the books recommended by friends and do not allow my thinking mind to edit the material that is drawn to me. Rather, I simply log into Amazon or head to the nearest bookstore and order it. At times, I have waited up to six months or a year before reading certain books I previously purchased.

Or, I may start a book immediately, only to put it down as I feel drawn to read another. In all instances, I am opening and expanding my awareness. Time passes and I connect with the content that I couldn't absorb several months earlier. Material that seemed impenetrable for weeks or months is now easily digested, and I wonder what stopped me previously from reading it. Sometimes it seems like I am reading a foreign language; at other times, the author's voice doesn't pull me in until I am ready to hear the message.

I then realize that the material reflects a higher frequency than I was used to at the time. It might be that my belief system was too rigid for me to expand and absorb it. In all cases, I stopped questioning why many years ago. Instead, I now consider it divine timing when my frequency is elevated in that "aha" moment to match that of the subject matter.

Sometimes I read four or five books in process at one time and alternate among the different frequencies contained in the books' messages. I feel alive and insightful as the material triggers energetic expansion and brings a truer awareness to me, guided at all times by my Inner Voice. Most joyous are the moments when it opens me up to a whole new way of looking at my experience. This is when a new pathway is activated within my consciousness and I feel so much growth.

Oftentimes I order material for friends who are not ready for its higher frequency, but my Inner Voice pushes me to do it, knowing that there will be a future frequency connection for them. It may be much later when I receive a call that they have just read the book with ease. I never question my inner guidance and its connection to their inner guidance because I have come to see that they will become more consciously aware in divine time.

Bejeweled Digits

Raising my frequency by reading higher-vibrational material, I have likewise raised the frequencies of my life experiences. Trusting my Inner Voice's guidance, I act within these frequencies despite the twisty-turny parts that my thinking mind can't begin to comprehend.

As a direct result of having raised my frequency in this way over the years, I have also attracted interesting and creative people into my life. One such couple has invited me several times to the Caribbean island of St. John to share a vacation house.

I had always wanted to visit this area, and on my first trip, I flew into St. Thomas two days early to read, relax, and look around. Once my friends arrived, I would meet them to take the ferry over to St. John.

Walking down the hill from my hotel for dinner that first night, I crossed a random street that was lined with jewelry stores as far as the eye could see. My thinking mind momentarily sneered in judgment of the volume of horse-trading that most likely occurred along that tourist trap.

Yet two days later, as I left a restaurant to meet my friends at the ferry, rising within me came a thought/feeling from my Inner Voice that I should buy an emerald ring. That day… immediately!

My thinking mind registered surprise and immediate resistance to the thought/feeling. It reasoned that over the past five years, I had felt drawn to the energy of an emerald ring several times. I had even once inquired about its cost at a New York jewelry store. But at this moment, my thinking mind insisted that I had only fifty-five minutes to head back to my hotel, check out, and wheel my bags down to the ferry. By all outer appearances, this idea was ludicrous!

My Inner Voice simply laughed and said, "Easy Peasy!" And with that, I rounded a corner to find myself on the street lined with jewelry stores that I had sneered at two nights earlier!

I felt some tension in my body as I began to act on my Inner Voice's direction and peer into store windows in search of a ring. All the while, my thinking mind continued to warn me that I had no idea how to even choose a "good" emerald.

My Inner Voice responded that I knew two things. First, that I could trust it to lead me in choosing my ring. Second, that I would spend around a thousand dollars.

While I mused that Elizabeth Taylor wouldn't have shopped for a gem at this price range, my Inner Voice reminded me that this process of purchasing and wearing the ring was really about elevating my frequency and being even more consciously aware. Wearing the energetic frequency that an emerald carries felt right.

At the third store, I felt drawn to an emerald ring with a price tag of one thousand eight hundred dollars. "Way out of YOUR budget," my thinking mind told me. And yet, I followed my Inner Voice's guidance as it twice directed me to begin walking out of the store during negotiations.

Within ten minutes, I was out the door with MY emerald ring. The final cost of my bling? One thousand fifty dollars! Thank you, thank you, Inner Voice!

As I made my way to the hotel and then the ferry with time to spare, my thinking mind remained shocked at what had transpired. Toward the end of my island adventure, it eventually came to accept my purchase, reasoning that this was an isolated incident driven by the joy of visiting a place about which I had always dreamed and doing so with great friends.

"Not so fast on the limiting thoughts," my Inner Voice chided me several days after I returned to New York. "You have nine other fingers. Time to visit the Manhattan Jewelry Exchange!" What?!

My thinking mind was apoplectic that I could even consider such an investment. Who could I trust to make such purchases amidst the immense warren of dealers in the Exchange District? How could I afford such extravagances? Who was I—a spiritual Liberace?

And yet I knew that my Inner Voice was pulling me into even higher frequencies that the additional stones on my fingers would bring. In fact, over the next nine weeks, I purchased nine additional rings from jewelers to whom my Inner Voice directed me.

While I can't say for certain that I can feel the higher frequencies that are present in the stones that adorn my fingers, I can attest that the synchronicities associated with living at a higher frequency significantly sped up around the time I purchased my tenth ring.

My income increased exponentially as the amount of effort I expended in my business proportionally decreased. New people and experiences simply materialized. In business deals, I was bumped twice, from last to first position as if by divine intervention. Creative ideas that would never have occurred to me before wearing the rings popped into my head like they had been there forever. New team members appeared at the precise moment that their skills were needed to complete and publish *Your Brilliant Inner Whisper*.

I have significantly relaxed as I work in the unknown of each day. My Inner Voice communication is clearer and more consistent than ever before. I no longer feel the need to control a person or an experience. Rather, I allow them to be revealed to me. Additional and more advanced reading material continues to flow to me that activates me to step into higher frequencies and new experiences.

I'm not saying that the energy field around my hands is strong enough to light my apartment if the electricity goes out. But I am grateful for being even more consciously aware and for living at and sustaining a higher frequency that continues to pull me forward.

◇◇◇

> *Reading higher-vibrational material may not result in bejeweled digits, but it will consistently activate you to explore ideas and experiences specific to your path that are tied to the higher frequencies of your dreams and desires.*

◇◇◇

Man relates to material things through direct insight rather than reason.

Immanuel Kant

Your Inner Voice in Action

Your Inner Whisper can pull you to the career and life expression you seek but were unable to find.

The rings' arrival symbolized a physical announcement of the significance of reaching the professional work I came to do in this lifetime.

They started arriving several weeks after I self-published my first book. I had used my hands to release the flow of information inside me into the physical.

With my awareness to bring a message of the Inner Voice's importance, I had stepped into a career path that I hadn't been able to find until in my fifties.

The answer to the question I had asked myself when I was eighteen—"How could I find a career that fit me like my father's suited him?"—had finally arrived. These gemstones were signs of the value of the product being mined within me.

My journey with the rings was extremely beneficial because it brought a huge life lesson of no longer looking for any approval outside myself. People were triggered in multiple ways by my wearing all these rings, and it became clear their reaction was none of my business.

However, I could not wear them while writing on the keyboard.... too much clicking and banging from hitting each other!

What personal or career expression are you being nudged to experience or pursue?

Chapter 22

Your Inner Voice and Outer Appearances

Whenever we find ourselves considering outer appearances, we can be assured that we are not connected to our Inner Voice. Instead, we are living above the neck in our thinking mind, without conscious awareness, and where outer appearances rule supreme.

Lacking Inner-Voice guidance, we cannot find or maintain the higher frequencies tied to our highest visions, and more than likely, we are numb or blindly pursuing mere distractions. The truth is that outer appearances are really nothing more than false appearances that distract us from the deeper truth of our path.

In most cases, neither our parents nor our teachers learned to use their Inner Voice as a valuable life tool, depriving future generations of its vital gifts. Consequently, we too have lacked the wisdom of this vast resource.

Lacking inner guidance, high school and college students now face a critical time in their lives for which they are vastly unprepared to make career decisions and may, in fact, be held hostage by outer appearances. Chaos and massive emotional stress ensue as they are blindly led by their thinking mind, unaware of an Inner Voice there to guide them to make those choices truest for their life's path.

Even those who currently work in unfulfilling careers might ask themselves if, upon tapping into their Inner Voice, they can revisit their lives since graduation and see NOW what did not seem possible THEN when the outer appearances seemed insurmountable.

The truth for all of us is that it is never too late to connect with our Inner Voice.

Vast numbers within our society live above the neck, numbing themselves to the frustration of being disconnected from their inner wisdom. Subjecting themselves to the chaos of outer appearances, they distract themselves with overspending, serial dating, TV, or overindulgence in sex, food, and liquor.

Wherever you may be in your life, NOW is the time to recognize that YOU are responsible for EVERYTHING in it.

Living from your Inner Voice causes a major shift in how the outer appearances look to you, and in fact, they begin to fall away to reveal your truth. Yes, there are always bills to pay. Jobs to work. Kids to manage responsibly. But you will be operating within an energetic pull from a place of strength and love deep within yourself that will be your guide.

You will step away from the unconscious herd when you stop doing what no longer fits you. As you gain clarity, your Inner Voice will lead you to create a set of beliefs customized to support YOU. Outer appearances will no longer have a stake in your daily decisions. Instead, they will merely serve to reflect back to you those issues or fears that you choose to release.

The Channeler

I recall far too many times when the outer appearances temporarily detained me on my journey as I fell prey to the chaos of my thinking mind. Failing to find resolution there, I would finally remember to go back down below the neck in search of my inner direction. Synchronicity would almost immediately ensue thereafter.

We are all blessed by those people we bring into our lives to help us look deeper inside ourselves. They are there to trigger us into a deeper conscious awareness through their presence, their words, their actions, or a combination of sorts. In many cases, we know the truth in those moments, although our thinking mind likens them to holding a wiggling rattlesnake in a bag.

One afternoon a woman, who I had come to know on her frequent visits to my Montana restaurant, walked in. Her youngest son worked for me, and she and I had always maintained a casual friendship filled with engaging conversations.

She was quite striking with a beauty that, at the time, I did not realize emanated from within her. Her physical beauty only magnified the effect. Her life force, or aura, was off the charts, although I could not have understood this concept at the time since I was not as spiritually aware of, nor as connected to, my Inner Voice.

That explains why I reacted the way I did one afternoon. She looked me straight in the eye and told me that she had just returned from a spiritual workshop where she had worked with a channeler, someone who can tune in to a plane other than the physical one in which we live and receive information. For the past month, she had this feeling that she should introduce me to this channeler. She released a nervous giggle as she shared this information.

Her statement caught me completely off guard. I recall my entire body tightening up and my breath becoming shallow. Time appeared to stand still. Talk about triggered!

Above the neck amidst the din in my thinking mind, I managed to respond to her in a clipped tone. "You definitely have the wrong guy because I don't even read my horoscope!"

Unfazed, she continued warmly. "Well, I have her number if you ever want it. You know where to reach me." She flashed that million-dollar smile, waved to junior, and off she went.

It wasn't until a few weeks later, after more than a few nights spent facing my resistance, that I finally went below the neck. Only then did I allow my Inner Voice to tell me that her words had triggered a deeper knowing that I had been ignoring.

Rather than face it, I had been distracted by the outer appearances of a high-living lifestyle, social friendships, and the illusion of financial security.

The truth of my reality, however, was that I had become bored with the restaurant. I was spiritually running on empty, deeply unhappy with my lack of personal growth, and unfulfilled with the life that I had worked for six years to create. Even worse, I didn't think I could stand to look at another taco without seeing a ball and chain tied to it. It was time for a change.

My Inner Voice told me exactly what I needed to do. I picked up the phone to dial my friend and ask for the introduction. The channeler provided a session filled with information that changed my life. And with that, the next door opened, leaving six years of outer appearances lying in the snow outside.

◇◇◇◇◇◇◇◇◇◇◇◇◇◇◇◇◇◇◇◇◇◇◇◇◇◇◇◇◇◇◇◇◇◇◇◇

Embrace those situations that are vitally important and divinely necessary to blow a hole in your boat filled with outer appearances, forcing you to get out and swim.

◇◇◇◇◇◇◇◇◇◇◇◇◇◇◇◇◇◇◇◇◇◇◇◇◇◇◇◇◇◇◇◇◇◇◇◇

People sometimes are so confident in their flawed beliefs that they get stuck – fixated – and as a result are blinded to insights that are right in front of them.

Gary A. Klein

Your Inner Voice in Action

> *Our Inner Voice helps us face another form of outer appearance: personal beliefs that don't fit us.*

I became aware of the strong barrier of resistance to my friend's suggestion to meet the channeler was because I was still holding onto my parents' religious beliefs. Her offer to meet was like an offer to dine with Satan.

I was in my late twenties and faced the glaring fact that I had done nothing to find a spiritual path of my own.

After the shock of her invitation dissipated, I started looking at how unhappy I was. I saw the religious beliefs I grew up with weren't me. The glaring proof was that I still had not faced the fact I was gay. I was holding religious beliefs that would not even allow me to pass through the pearly gates. I suddenly had a lot of personal honesty and rebooting directly in my face.

Within several weeks of soul-searching, my Inner Voice finally had a toe hold and nudged me to accept the invitation to meet the channeler.

The chandler turned out to be a significant life-fork to seek personal spiritual tools for expanding my life.

I have seen that when we start acting on our Inner Voice's nudges, we will be pulled to spiritual information that speaks to us.

Writing this story breakdown caused me to question why so many of us hold our parents' beliefs even though it's glaringly evident they do not fit our lives?

> What beliefs are you holding that no longer fit your life but that you haven't yet addressed?

Chapter 23

Your Inner Voice and Someone Else's Rules

Someone else's rules offer opportunities for us to take action that brings us closer to who we are and what we came here to do. Our Inner Voice makes us aware of the resistance we may have against it.

Someone else's rules do not feel true to us, as though they violate some inner knowing we have. They also may reflect a personality behind the rules with which we feel uncomfortable. In many instances, someone else's rules will cause us to expand past our comfort zone as we work to liberate ourselves from their influence.

Whatever they reflect, we may resist someone else's rules by shutting down and becoming unconscious. Or by reacting in anger and frustration and feeling controlled and manipulated. Or by acting the role of a victim as though we have no choice in the matter. Either way, we are resisting the need to be consciously aware and move forward.

Yet someone else's rules are really a two-fold blessing as they activate our Inner Voice to (1) tell us that we are headed in a direction that feels true for us, or (2) trigger us to face the fact that those choices are no longer a fit for us. The gift they offer us is clarity, as our Inner Voice directs us to move forward either way.

Many people are conditioned to follow someone else's rules to feel safe, rather than embrace the truth that security exists only within us and not outside of us as the outer appearances falsely represent. They hate their jobs (or a situation), complaining, or feeling victimized, instead of changing jobs or finding a new career (or resolution). They are unwilling to take responsibility in the form of Inner Voice-directed action that could otherwise lead them away from where they don't want to be.

Someone else's rules apply to career professionals who follow a specific path (medical, law, finance), which offers little chance for them to connect to their Inner Voice and create a structure for its practice and development. They voice frustration that they feel unfulfilled. Or wish they had room for the stretch of new experiences, and perhaps, that they had chosen a totally different path.

Even after they retire, they may fail to hear the calls of their Inner voice having spent their entire lives in their thinking minds and tuned only into the outer appearances.

Military careers are similarly constrained by someone else's rules due to the rigid boundaries (that are required) and conditions experienced by those who join its ranks. Those considering a military career would be better prepared to choose this path if they first learn to hear, trust, and act on their Inner Voice direction to know whether or not it is a true fit for them.

Many of the men and women who serve our country are, in fact, left stranded (and feel abandoned) when they finish their tour of duty. There is no Inner Voice education in place to help them create their personal rules as they reintegrate into nonmilitary careers, where they are unaccustomed to the lack of someone else's rules to guide them.

Be especially aware of someone else's rules governing those who you entrust authority. Do not discount your Inner Voice's resistance to professional advice that doesn't feel right to you. Don't allow someone with more education than you to bulldoze what you know to be true inside! Follow your Inner Voice's guidance.

Regardless of why we have been living by someone else's rules, NOW is the time to recognize that we are the ones who have allowed the rules to keep us from our passions, dreams, and personal expression in so many areas.

We may never have been taught to make creative expression a priority in our lives. Nor were we taught to trust ourselves from the inside out. Still, it is our responsibility to make our Inner Voice a priority if we are going to create a life that best reflects our personal truth.

Singing at the College National Finals Rodeo

I was not always consciously aware enough to act consistently on my Inner Voice's guidance, especially in my earlier years. My thinking mind insisted on managing my daily choices and career plans, including my decision to become a singer after I sold my restaurant. "After all," it thought from above the neck. "I have a good voice and years of vocal training to support me!"

My thinking mind just knew that it could connect the dots to achieve my goal by booking a singing gig at the College National Finals Rodeo held in the same town where my restaurant was located. Using my connections, I could secure a singing contract at the rodeo venue, and I would soon croon to thousands of rodeo fans on my way to an overnight success story!

I booked the gig. I would open the rodeo finals singing the "Star-Spangled Banner" and perform several other songs that evening, followed by two additional evenings of performances. I was on my way!

It came together so easily that at the time I might have thought it was my Inner Voice running the show. However, at the time I was still unaware of the term and the power of its guidance, other than a few key moments when it had previously surfaced along my path.

The debacle that followed serves as an example of how we confuse circumstances of allowing our thinking mind to connect the dots versus our Inner Voice to guide us.

The day before my debut, the leader of the band (hired by the rodeo venue) told me there was no time to rehearse our set. While I experienced an immediate inner knowing that this was unacceptable, I wasn't tuned in enough to my fledgling Inner Voice to hear and act on its guidance to stand up to someone else's rules. Instead, my thinking mind simply rationalized that everything would work out. Hadn't it been easy thus far?

The next evening as the band played the opening notes, I began to sing the "National Anthem" standing on a dais in the arena gazing out at ten thousand people with their hands on their hearts and eyes on the flag. The first few words rang out from me in perfect timing to the band's accompaniment… until THAT moment when I realized I had no clue where they were in the music.

And so, I stopped singing.

And the band kept playing.

And I found myself staring out at ten thousand people who had turned their gaze from our nation's flag to stare back at me. For what seemed to be an infinite number of agonizing moments, we stared at each other until the band played out the last notes.

I descended from the dais and walked across the arena and out of the gate never to return. It was the longest walk of shame that I have ever known.

I was fired the next day from the rest of the engagement. So much for connecting the dots.

For years afterward, the hair on the back of my neck would stand up whenever my thinking mind looked back to that night. It was the last, ego-fueled circumstance that it ever orchestrated. Even IT knows it doesn't like to live through epic failure!

When someone else's rules don't work for you, let your Inner Voice do the talking. Had I been more deeply rooted in its wisdom, I would never have accepted the "no" that I could not rehearse the entire set before the performance. My Inner Voice knew I needed a rehearsal, but that inner knowing was trumped by my thinking mind's need to connect the dots, adhere to someone else's rules, and rationalize that all was well in the outer appearances. Never again!

Your Inner Voice will help you to create the personal rules that you need to walk your truest path.

A point of view can be a dangerous luxury when substituted for insight and understanding.

Marshall McLuhan

Your Inner Voice in Action

Gaining skill handling your ego while enforcing personal and professional boundaries

Singing at the rodeo finals is still the most embarrassing moment of my life. My ego felt like an eighteen-wheeler had run over it with an audience in attendance.

This situation raised the bar on how high I could ascend in personal humiliation!

The plus side of learning from my crushed ego was that I was clear from this point forward. I would stand up to anyone if I needed them to show up to fulfill a commitment I had made.

I no longer allow my thinking mind to connect the dots to create something for my ego's gain. Now, every project I make is Inner-Voice directed.

A few years after this nightmare, my dad sent me an article that listed all the famous singers who had gotten lost in the accompaniment while singing the "Star-Spangled Banner."

Retelling the story to an audience, I can fully join in their laughter at this life teaching. I've had numerous people say I helped them start releasing their own scorching embarrassment by sharing my experience.

This moment had a massive benefit for increasing my ability to set both personal and professional boundaries.

> Think of a situation when your ego and thinking mind got burned for connecting the dots, instead of basing your decision on the Inner Whisper within.

Chapter 24

Your Inner Voice Is God within You

Some people don't like to hear the word "God." For many years, I was one of them. Youthful experiences tied to that three-letter word can be so painful that they go numb when God's name is invoked. I certainly don't judge them on it, especially since I no longer live in my thinking mind.

If you find yourself in that place, I encourage you to transition past the pain you carry from someone else's rules about God that were pushed on you earlier in your life. Trust your Inner Voice to guide you toward the spiritual practice and reading material that best works for you at this stage in your journey.

Experiences like when God is pushed on you may seem all too familiar. A neighbor praises God during a play date with their child or never misses a chance to quote the Bible across the fence. Your coworker tells you indignantly that her God is the real one. Your parent used the specter of God's wrath to control you as a child.

Even using terms like "New Age" and "spiritual" in light conversation may result in righteous anger from those who judge your beliefs as being out of alignment with theirs.

The great news is that you now trust yourself to make your decisions through your Inner Voice. Consequently, you are free to choose a name for God that is a fit for you. This is your truth!

There are infinite possibilities including, but certainly not limited to Higher Power, Source, Creator, Guide, Angel, Ascended Master, Higher Self, God Self, Divine Mind, I AM, Invisible Assistance, Higher Guidance, Highest Good, or Best Friend. The energy associated with any one of these labels is the same; it is an awareness of a connection to higher assistance.

The more I trust my Inner Voice to lead me, the more consciously aware I am that I have always had higher assistance to help me connect to what I want in my life. Years passed before I fully cleansed myself of the rigid views that were imposed upon me by someone else's rules about God in my youth.

Singing in Church

One week during college break, my mother approached me (yet again) with her sales pitch that I should sing in church at the upcoming Sunday service. I was surprised because I had made it clear that singing in front of her people was definitely not one of my desires. However, when her pitch turned to the plea, "But we never get to hear you sing anymore!" my thinking mind caved in.

I did stand my ground on one point in our negotiation. My good friend (who was also well-liked by my family) would accompany me on the piano in place of the church pianist, who at times was heavy-handed on the ivories. She often lagged so far behind the vocalist that I wondered if she had gone home to God and her fingers were the only thing left in this dimension.

Thrilled at her successful negotiation, my mother flew to the phone to share the wondrous news with the minister that her son would be singing in church that Sunday. At the mention of my friend accompanying me, however, I watched her face contort. Her mouth dropped open, and her brow furrowed as the minister told her that he could not have my friend play the piano because she went to another church. And THAT conflicted with HIS religious (and apparently God's) convictions!

My mother was stunned. The minister of her church (my folks were founding members) was telling her that God didn't want our family friend to play the piano because she attended a different church? I inwardly wondered if my friend knew that she could now add the word "sinner" to her resume!

That phone call was a shock to my mother, especially since we had so many close friends and neighbors of various faiths. Explaining that her pastor's position was a perfect example of why I had never wanted to pass over his threshold, I emphasized that God's right-hand man had missed an opportunity to convert my friend to his faith. I pictured her trapped in the front pew, silently enduring his forty-five-minute sermon, as the wind passed over his vocal cords directly into her face. I likened it to sitting directly in front of a fan with the speed set way too high!

Needless to say, I did not sing in church that Sunday. Nor did my mother ever ask me to attend church again.

I believe at that moment on the phone with the pastor, my mother felt a shift as her Inner Voice revealed the cracks in the rigid dogma of someone else's rules that no longer fit her.

*As you connect to your Inner Voice,
you connect to higher assistance. Name it anything
you want. Never again will you question its place
in your life as you revel in its strength.*

Don't let the noise of others' opinions drown out your own Inner Voice.

Steve Jobs

Your Inner Voice in Action

> *Our Inner Voice pulls us to see others "when they show us who they are," therefore allowing them their convictions.*

The minister's decision clarified to me and my parents that I would no longer attend their church, which was a huge relief.

Cutting this religious cord offered freedom I had needed for a very long time. So, in the end, the pastor's conviction had done me a huge favor!

After the church skirmish, my parents stepped back with an upgraded but bruised clarity. Their more neutral support has been invaluable because it allows me to comfortably engage with a wide range of people with different beliefs.

Most importantly, I have a greater understanding that I only have control of one life, my own; therefore, it's none of my business to judge others' spiritual or religious convictions.

> Do you have people in your life you're resisting because you don't want to accept their truth when they are showing you who they are?

Chapter 25

Speaking from Your Inner Voice

SOMETIMES WHEN I speak with someone, I remain filled for a while with the Inner Voice energy that rose through me during the conversation.

The current is so strong that it can feel like I am plugged into an electrical outlet. As I speak, I become aware of this powerful frequency that spreads throughout my body.

The other day I called a friend to ask a question. Early into the conversation, I became aware of a higher energetic frequency rooted in my Inner Voice that came through my speaking voice as I shared what I felt my friend needed to hear. Similar to speaking with passion, it has a different feel and energy that carries a ring of truth in the center of the message. I also became aware of a shift within my friend as she heard the truth in the message and felt its energetic pull.

Speaking-voice energy that emanates from your Inner Voice is not used to persuade someone to agree with you. Rather, it is so firmly rooted in your truth that, like it or not, your subject will hear the insightful information as it comes from that higher source, passing through you and out of your mouth. The information is always based on truth, and it is what they are ready to hear, whether they are aware of it or not. You are merely the conduit.

And, yes, at times you are meant to hear the message for your own good too.

What's most exhilarating about this level of energy flow is that you will suddenly feel inspired in your life by a truthful idea that you find yourself sharing with another person in conversation.

Once you are in the flow of this speaking-voice energy, you are no longer aware of being tired, hungry, on a tight schedule, or of any other personal needs. In most instances, you are only partially aware of what you are saying. Sometimes your thinking mind may even have to play catchup with the conversation! Time stands still, and the moment is only about the truth of the message being delivered.

It's not so much the tenor or volume of your voice as it is the frequency tied to what you say. People simply feel this energy as it activates them on some level, regardless of whether it appears to register with them. It is of no concern to you how or what they hear from you. That would otherwise be your thinking mind stepping in to judge their reaction. No. Stay below the neck in these moments.

Remember that when speaking from your Inner Voice with another, your thinking mind plays no role; you are NOT the doer, only a vessel. The message should be delivered with absolute and unconditional love and not from ego or with any expected outcome.

From this same place that has guided you first to your truth, you will also receive guidance to help activate and awaken someone else to their truth. What a wondrous feeling we experience in these moments!

Hauling Straw Bales

While it would be several years beyond the age of seventeen before I would recognize and understand the words "Inner Voice," nonetheless I felt it grow stronger in my daily life even then. I felt it both within me and in the way I spoke with my family and with strangers around me. At times it seemed I was speaking from a deeper place I was unaccustomed to and, in many instances, completely unaware of.

One afternoon my brother and I were hauling truckloads of straw bales that Dad had sold to one of our neighbors. Five years my senior, my brother always tried to run the show according to his personal schedule; in this case, dictating to me that we should add an additional tier of bales per load. Driven purely by his thinking mind to finish more quickly, perhaps to impress Dad, he recklessly disregarded Dad's instructions on the number of bales per load that we could safely haul.

Consequently, my brother overloaded the bales on the truck despite my protestations. I knew that we were headed for trouble. As we approached a hill, I gently reminded him that we should at least keep the truck to the center of the road, so it didn't lean and lose part of our load down over the bank. But you couldn't tell him anything. Certainly, my seventeen years of experience on this earth was of no value to him, so my repeated warning of the danger ahead went unheeded.

And then it happened. We took the curve too sharply and lost a big chunk of bales off the side of the load and down over a steep bank. As we walked back to peer over the edge, I saw that many of the bales were stopped by a fence that clung to the hillside. What a mess. And then my brother uttered the words that awakened a new level of my Inner Voice. He told me that WE had better get started hauling the bales up over the bank!

It seemed in that moment that time stood still. In reaction to his barked orders, my Inner Voice suddenly and powerfully activated as though it had been lifting weights for years and never tested its strength. I responded to him in such a manner and in such clarity that I think it shocked both of us. In that moment of speaking MY inner truth, my brother became aware of a power in me he had never experienced, even as I became aware of it myself. As I came to understand later, it had been growing within me all those years.

My Inner Voice told him that he was now going to take full responsibility for his willful decisions and disregard of my warnings. It continued to inform him that HE was going to haul every bale up that bank by himself. Finally, I heard myself telling him that I was walking back to the closest neighbor, calling Mom to pick me up. Then I was going to drive into town and see a movie!

Even as he jumped around, cursing and yelling at me to get back there, we both knew that things had changed forever between us. My speaking-voice energy had never been stronger than in those moments, and my words had never been so eloquent. I laughed as I walked away thinking he shouldn't be wasting his energy jumping around and yelling about the mess he had to clean up.

When I recounted the situation to my parents, they heard the shift in me too, and the three of us had a good laugh at my brother's comeuppance.

Until that moment, I had no idea of the impact that the speaking-voice energy from my Inner Voice would have on another person until it flexed its power within me that afternoon. The voice inside me was strong enough to stand up to the unconscious (and outrageous) behavior based upon someone else's rules.

My Inner Voice taught me that I was strong enough to speak my truth and no longer tolerate or accept my brother's behavior. It was indeed a defining moment in my life. And I suppose my brother's life as well.

◇◇

Speaking from our Inner Voice conveys our deepest truths and activates the truths within those to whom we speak.

◇◇

Your Inner Voice whispers but speaks the loudest.

Matshona Dhliwayo

Your Inner Voice in Action

> *Inner Voice-directed eloquence brings*
> *a powerful clarity to any conversation.*

My Inner Voice directed a life-altering force and truth with my brother that changed our future dealings. There was no going back.

From this point forward, the whisper within me would be my most assertive advocate when trusting myself to stand my ground on a personal level.

I look back on that day of verbal clarity, knowing it originated from the same place of activation as when I invited Dr. Mannion to lunch and when I had the vocal power to convince my father to finance a restaurant. It was also the underlying power in writing the letter to the landlord requesting a two-bedroom.

Releasing this powerful flow of your Inner Voice up through you will change every area of your life.

> Can you remember a time when you felt the power of the Inner Whisper come up through you to aid you in a conversation?

Chapter 26

Your Inner Voice is Your Personal GPS

In an earlier chapter, I mentioned that working with your Inner Voice and frequency is like moving up and down the radio dial and tuning into different stations. You can't see the radio frequencies, and yet, you know that something must be there to carry the music that you can hear. When you place your coffee cup in the microwave, you don't see the microwaves at work, but after a minute or so your coffee emerges piping hot.

Inner-Voice energy works the same way. I can't see the energy connected to it any more than I can see a radio frequency or a microwave. But I feel the energy as it pulls/pushes me, and I enjoy tangible results when I honor it.

It is my personal GPS, a radar guidance system that is specific to my life path.

Are you ready to stop resisting what you can't see? Consider the "Dark Night of The Soul" situations that many of you may face at some point in your life when you feel overwhelmed by credit card debt, unemployment, or an aloneness with no one to love.

These are the watershed moments when you face a fork in your road. Are you willing to finally go below the neck and allow your Inner Voice to serve as your personal GPS to show you the way out of your current situation? Even though you can't see it and may not yet even be able to feel it?

If you find yourself resisting as you read this, you are still above the neck in your thinking mind. Our thinking mind resistance tells us that it doesn't exist if we can't see it, touch it, or hear it. Or that it is not real if it isn't instant gratification. How easily we forget that our troubled situations took months or years to accrue, and yet we expect instant relief!

Resistance goes hand in hand with anything new and unfamiliar. We won't try a new dessert that tastes different or wear a new shade of purple that we were attracted to on the rack. Or break our routine. Our thinking mind is still running the show. Now is when we can choose to go inside and look to our personal GPS for help.

Working below the neck and above the waist, you no longer allow your thinking mind to tell you that it will take five years to pay off the credit cards. Or worry about how to conduct your job search. Or whether you will find a partner. Or that you must plan before you act. You will never again have to ask who, what, where, when, how, or why. These are all terms used by the thinking mind to distract you from relying on your personal GPS.

Just stop resisting challenges by overthinking or ignoring them. By looking at them. By complaining about them. Don't allow your thinking mind to judge, edit, or control your actions. Instead, hear, trust, and act on your Inner Voice guidance.

Call the credit card companies to acknowledge the debt and set up the minimum payment plan, trusting that your inner guidance will lead you toward the solution that works for you.

Search the internet for the job categories that interest you. Share with your friends, family, or strangers the information describing the job that you want.

Sign up for an online dating site. Join more than one. Write out a profile of who you are and who your mate is.

In that moment, you will cross over that invisible line of resistance.

Trust that your personal GPS will pull you forward as your life opens up in front of you. Your Inner Voice has all the strength, love, and power to support you. Trust the divine radar guidance system that is your personal GPS.

There were many days that all I could do was acknowledge my highest vision for this book and then sit down at the computer to face my thinking mind's resistance. In every instance, it simply evaporated. It will for you too.

Trusting My Personal GPS

The morning that I felt inexplicably pulled to drop my college classes, put on my ski clothes, and hop in the car for the drive up to the ski hill, I chose to honor the pull of my personal GPS.

In those early days, I skied mogul after mogul as my personal GPS pulled me forward in the direction of who I am and what I came here to do. I fluctuated daily between below-the-neck elation and above-the-neck dread as my radar guidance system led me further away from the herd mentality of my classmates. I saw them in the evenings and regaled them with my day's adventures, but I could not share with them the turmoil that I felt inside. I had never known such a solitary existence.

In subzero temperatures, I skied daily, alone, and in the chaos of my Thinking Mind's confusion and self-doubt. What would I tell my father? What would I do for money when it ran out? What was I thinking? My bumps and spills seemed to shake up feelings of paralyzing fear and overwhelming guilt that surfaced up into my thinking mind.

Yet, in time, I learned to trust the feeling of my Inner Voice's pull. I felt its power growing inside of me as I was led in a direction away from the chaos and fear of my thinking mind as it considered the outer appearances. Although I wasn't aware of it then, this inner power and the freedom that appeared with it (and no homework!) was part of my personal GPS-directed road map. It was programmed and locked onto my future highest visions.

Throughout that semester, I never once considered going back to class, thanks to the support of my personal GPS. All these years later, it has guided me right up to writing these pages in anticipation of sharing my Inner Voice journey with you.

That winter alone on the hill, my personal GPS guided me in a direction that was the truest fit for who I am and what I came here to do.

Listen to your Inner Voice. It is the calling of your spiritual GPS system seeking to keep you on track toward your true destiny.

Anthon St. Maarten

EREC LINDBERG

Your Inner Voice in Action

> *Your true north is always anchored within your Inner Voice;*
> *it's still your most accurate GPS.*

The day I chose my Inner-Voice-directed GPS to quit my classes over the fear, alarm, and warning of my thinking mind is still the most crucial decision of my life.

It changed the direction of my life. I was not supposed to be sitting in classrooms that winter. My life-path education was to gain trust in the whisper within me while having two boards on my feet with snow under them.

There has not been a day of regret in quitting my classes. As I've shared, I did continue with a pre-med focus, but once again, from a soul-directed GPS, my Inner Voice pointed me in a more authentic direction.

I have not shared how I faced my father at the end of the quarter. I tried to write three letters. But I could not convey my inner process in writing to justify quitting my classes, nor was I strong enough to stand in my new beliefs.

In the end, I told him I wasn't doing well with my classes, and my advisor suggested I drop them so I wouldn't lower my GPA. You might think this was a lie, but I was aware this was something my father could hear and grudgingly accept. At that time, I knew this was enough.

Years later, when I owned a restaurant and we were sitting on the beach in Mexico during our Christmas holiday, I told Dad the whole story. I let the eloquence of my Inner Voice flow up through me. When I finished, my father shook his head and started laughing. I took this as proof that it will all work out when people are ready to hear the truth of an Inner Voice delivery.

> What are you aware of that your GPS is pulling you toward right now in your life?

Chapter 27

Your Inner Voice and Living in Abundance

Following your Inner Voice's guidance will provide you with an abundance flow with which you are matched in frequency at any given moment. When I speak of abundance flow, I mean timing, relationships, connections, introductions, and personal shifts, in addition to financial abundance, that are integral parts of a greater divine web of synchronicity.

Abundance flow is part of the greater whole that is you working at all levels within yourself and with your surrounding environment. It includes personal growth, raised conscious awareness, and the inner clarity that best reflects the abundance that you seek to attract.

As you hear, trust, and act on your Inner Voice's guidance, you will gain a sense of how it feels to experience the pull of abundance flow. The more you fully trust your Inner Voice's guidance, the more abundance flow you will experience.

The more I have come to hear, trust, and act on my Inner Voice's guidance, the closer I have also come to the edge of my comfort zone where my thinking mind cannot begin to plan when, where, and how my abundance flow will appear. In fact, I learned years ago to simply let go of my thinking mind's expectations or need to connect the dots.

I have come to understand and accept that I am not the doer in my life. Rather, I am simply following my Inner Voice's directions, and in my experience of abundance flow, the bills get paid as I continue to achieve my highest visions.

While everything works out in divine timing, I have also come to understand that the outcome has nothing to do with the process, much less my asserting control over it. Nor does the outcome always resemble any expectations my thinking mind might anticipate. Rather, I fully trust and accept that my Inner Voice has led me through a process and to an outcome that is divinely intended as my abundance flow.

For example, you may feel that being debt-free is the abundance flow that you seek. If you are working only from your thinking mind, your desire to be debt-free may simply be a need that originated as the result of past guilt or pain connected to old spending patterns or being controlled by someone who held the purse strings. You may perceive that being debt-free will make you happy. In all these instances, your thinking mind is focused solely on outer appearances.

However, until you drop below the neck to work with your Inner Voice, you may never realize that being debt-free may not truly reflect who you are. Nor may it reflect who you are regarding your highest visions. I have several relatives and acquaintances who have no debt AND no sense of who they are or what they came here to do. In fact, they are miserable most of the time in their debt-free lives.

Abundance flow that is tied to your Inner Voice's guidance may be either debt-free living or living with high, manageable stress-free debt. In either case, it will be abundance that truly reflects who you are and what you came here to do.

Earnest Money or Dental Work

When I made an offer to purchase my first house, my real estate broker (who was also a spiritually inclined friend) knew that I didn't have all of the earnest money deposit in my bank account when I submitted the offer to the seller. Acting in her professional capacity, she felt obligated to go above the neck and speak to me. She sternly said, "This is serious because this contract is a legal document."

Being clear that I was acting from my Inner Voice's guidance, however, I told her to proceed with submitting the offer. And then we waited. No response from the seller for months.

Yet over those months, I lived within an abundance flow I knew was tied to the house purchase. Guided by my Inner Voice at every step, I knew the money was all there for the closing. By the time the contract was accepted and the closing date set, I had the full amount of the earnest money deposit physically in my account.

Then, a month before closing I was faced with an unexpected dental emergency that took half of my accumulated deposit. I became tense as I jumped into my thinking mind. However, I had made the offer due to the direction of my Inner Voice, and it continued to feel true for me, so I just quickly dropped back down below the neck and trusted in continued abundance flow.

A week or so after the dental work, I called a friend who I hadn't seen for some time. During our conversation, I mentioned my unexpected dental bills since she completely understands such expenses. Without any prompting by me or mention of my scheduled house closing, she suddenly said, "I just sold my apartment. Do you need a loan for your upcoming closing?

I'm happy to do it!" And here was the abundance flow divinely guided by my Inner Voice!

I have come to understand that invoices are always paid in divine time on those purchases that are tied to commitments I make when I act on my Inner Voice's guidance. In this instance, my abundance flow supplied me with additional funds to repay the loan soon after the closing and with interest that my friend hadn't required or expected.

◇◇

Your abundance flow is directly tied to the frequency of who you are regarding the frequency of that abundance.

◇◇

If you have some idea you believe in, don't listen to the croaking chorus. Listen only to what your own Inner Voice tells you.

Dale Carnegie

Your Inner Voice in Action

I offer this story of supply to bring this book full circle. In Chapter One, I shared my fear to mail a request to the landlord that resulted in a signed apartment lease in my dream location.

This final story proves the money was supplied following the dental expense. So once again, my Inner Voice brought the perfect home into my hands when I was ready for my next place to live.

When we trust and act on our Inner Voice, the supply is always connected, right from the beginning of its energetic nudge to action.

After renovating my train-station home, it was featured in three magazines and became a salon for the area. There were times I would host up to three hundred people for fundraising gatherings.

I share my Inner Voice-directed journey of this house coming into my hands in my second book, **THE WHISPER TO CREATE, *The Nudge of Higher Assistance Surrounding Each of Us.***

Let's just say this second book involves a lot of twisty-turny parts before this fantastic property came into my hands and that my Inner Voice handled every unexpected turn.

Thank You for taking this journey with me.

If you are interested in my coaching services or finding out about my mastermind classes or keynote bookings, please contact me through my website ErecLindberg.com or by email at ErecLindberg@yahoo.com.

My best wishes to you for your incredible Inner-Voice journey forward!

Afterword

Living in the Flow of Your Inner Voice

You did it! You have completed the journey. You have unearthed your greatest possession that lies below the neck and found the courage to listen to its voice. By following my story about this exciting process, yours is about to unfold.

Your Brilliant Inner Whisper has activated you to trust yourself below the neck and above the waist to live from your Inner Voice's guidance. Now, in essence, you have stepped "out" of your thinking mind to live in the flow of your inner voice. You are closer to discovering who you are and what you came here to do.

You are now on your way to becoming self-sustaining with trusting the inner you on your life path. (This is Inner Voice speak for "living off the inner grid.") Watch what happens and be prepared to see miracles blossom in your life!

As you relax into this inner process, you will begin to feel and know that life challenges big or small will be handled. Your thinking mind will become aware of this feeling. It will remain calm and connected to this inner sense without the need to override it or connect the dots.

You will no longer feel angst as you face the vast unknown. You will no longer feel lost, hopeless, overwhelmed, and or confused. Instead, you will continue to expand your conscious awareness of all that is true for you, drawing new and enriching experiences into your life.

By reading this book and taking this journey with me—through my triumphs in following my Inner Voice and even my failures in ignoring it—you have gained an invaluable tool to carry you on your life's path that will always serve you in the best and highest manner.

But wait, there's more. We all know, as works-in-progress, that this represents a lifelong learning adventure. So, as your coach, I'm still here to help you every step of the way.

My second book, *THE WHISPER TO CREATE,* is nearing completion. In its pages, I also share more personal stories, including information that I have only told a few people about… among them, a turn of events that happened immediately following Nora Ephron's passing, which was higher assistance-directed and kept nudging my Inner Voice for over forty-eight hours.

In this upcoming book, I also reveal, through a three-year segment of my life, how everything is connected and higher-assistance directed. It started as a comment to a friend in my Montana restaurant that I would like to crew on a sailboat. Three years later it resulted in getting the last seat for a show in a New York cabaret club. This three-year string of continuous higher-assisted string events culminated in another pivotal fork in my life, serving as a prime example of this process in action.

Where do we go from here?

You and I may not face Lewis and Clark's physical challenges as they explored the vast Western frontier. We are, however, inner explorers who face the last great frontier within each of us.

We can no longer be sleepers. We face a critical point on this planet as we do in our inner development. We must decide if we are willing to raise our conscious awareness to better confront our global and inner challenges. We must set out now into the vast unknown within us. There are valuable gifts inside each of us that the world needs.

Your Brilliant Inner Whisper has prepared you to be consciously aware of what is resonating within you! What choices are you ready to make based on those prompts and nudges rising up from within you? So, are you going to saddle the horse or just watch the rodeo? Are you on the sidelines or are you in the game?

Hear, trust, and act on your Inner Voice guidance as you stand in the light of who you are and what you came here to do.

Visit www.ErecLindberg.com to learn more about the Inner Voice journey, find more suggestions for additional Inner Voice-related material, and share your personal experiences.

Join your fellow Inner-Voice enthusiasts at **Your Brilliant Inner Whisper**, a private Facebook Group where I share this Inner Voice-directed wisdom.

Register here to receive a special notice when **The Whisper to Create** is released!

Contact me at info@ereclindberg.com if you are interested in Inner Voice-directed coaching sessions. Or just write me to share your amazing experiences after reading mine and following the prompts from your Inner Voice.

It's time to reach for your highest visions…and I can't wait to hear your glorious stories!

Tribute

In Memory of Jane Bishoff

My dear friend, Jane Bishoff, sadly passed away before she could hold a copy of *Your Brilliant Inner Whisper* in her hands. There are moments I can still feel her influence in its pages.

Through our eleven years of friendship, Jane consistently encouraged me to listen to my Inner Voice and to keep writing.

In our often direct and laughter-filled conversations, she would remind me how important it was to get the message of *Your Brilliant Inner Whisper* out into the world. She shared her personal journey and the obstacles she overcame in her early years with the help of her Inner Voice as it guided her through those challenges.

She truly believed that everyone should be taught how to hear, trust, and act on their Inner Voice's guidance and that it could well be the greatest gift they might ever receive.

Jane stood in the center of the word YES. Whenever I hosted a community gathering, her reply was always the same: "YES, of course, Richard and I will be there," followed by "Can we do anything to help?"

Jane and Richard, her loving husband of thirty-five years, emotionally supported me when I made the decision to sell my beloved Montana home.

It wasn't long before I got the call from Jane informing me that, from now on, I was to consider their home to be my new Montana home. She always ensured that I had a vehicle to drive on my visits, even after I mangled the front end of her SUV. I am so deeply grateful for those times spent with them.

Jane and Richard, you were a team who always had my back. Thank you for your commitment to help me and to help others say YES to our Inner Voices.

Jane, you are deeply loved and greatly missed by all of us. You shall never be forgotten, and your memory lives on forever in *Your Brilliant Inner Whisper.*

Acknowledgments

From the heart center of who I am, I express my love and gratitude to everyone who has supported me in the birth of this book.

I am deeply grateful to my extraordinary editor, Catherine J. Rourke, for bringing her extensive skills and Inner Voice to this work. Known as "The Editorial Intuitive," she used her brilliant Inner Whisper to guide her wordsmithing in synergetic orchestration with me as a collaborative team. I was enthralled by the innate sense of clarity and creativity she brought to every aspect of my book as she helped me craft a smooth and expressive transitional flow.

I have come to see Catherine as an editor's editor—a literary powerhouse who draws from her Oxford education and decades of staff experience at major publishing houses, daily newspapers, and national magazines plus her strategic copywriting expertise developed from years of corporate communications. She has injected this book with her wisdom and mastery from cover to cover, handling it with talent, poise, and an incredible zest for life. Most importantly, she has become my dear and trusted friend!

To my dear friend, Kathy Greidanus, for your generous encouragement, supportive input, and deep respect for my highest visions. You were always the insightful sounding board for me.

To Glenda Hanna, for your supportive influence in my life since childhood. Thank you for your insightful proofreading and heartfelt input at the eleventh hour. Your friendship remains invaluable.

Your Brilliant Inner Whisper has benefited greatly from the wisdom and generosity of many others: Danit Almog, Claudia Alt, Jack and Lynn Anderson, Ann Bellwood, Vivian Bridaham, Rolf Burgi, Adrianna Cohen, Tom Crisp, Patti Cuttler, Hali Fleming, Ann Fleuchaus, Cyndi Fonda, Doug Freeman, Coats Guiles, Sandy Johnson, Patricia Kuhn, Nancy Lindberg, Kimberly Errington Moers, Nola and Jerry Mosher, Bill and Linda Musser, Lisa Nicoll, Julie Petersen, Tom Newbury and Tom Sandon, Susanne Phelps, Stephanie Rivera, Susan Rockefeller, Anne-Marie Rolfe, Ardis Scott, Paul Sheenan, Celeste Simone, Lisa Tener, Joyce Van Baak, Marian Waddems, and Robin Wilcox.

Also, my heartfelt thanks to the late Dr. Mannion and Dr. Steve Kritsick.

Finally, to Elizabeth Gilbert, Neale Donald Walsch, and Napoleon Hill for bringing their work into the world by listening to their Inner Voice.

ABOUT THE AUTHOR
EREC LINDBERG

Motivational author, coach, and speaker Erec Lindberg helps individuals and groups clarify their power and purpose by reuniting them with their most significant asset, their Inner Voice.

Sharing his wisdom through uplifting and often hilarious true stories, Erec shows people how to discover their Inner Voice and harness their inner power.

As a professional life coach, he guides clients worldwide to make positive choices based on the most authentic reflection of who they are and what they came here to achieve…by hearing, trusting, and acting on their Inner Voice and integrating it into their daily lives.

The Montana native has pursued every interest that ever called to him—a direct result of heeding his Inner Voice, which he discovered in his teens. Living between an apartment off Manhattan's Central Park and a renovated train-station home overlooking the Montana Rockies featured in three magazines, Erec owned and operated a boutique catering business for New York's rich and famous.

This Inner Voice influencer now resides with his dog Razz, a mini-Australian Shepherd, in a small studio in southern Oregon, keeping life simple so he can honor the powerful pull of his Inner Voice to finish writing his second book and serve as a guide for readers around the world.

But Erec never dwelled in the mundane or clung to comfort zones.

His high-adrenaline pursuits included working with horses, ranking him among the Top Ten riders in the nation in Working Cow Horse events and as Montana's All-Around Rider for two consecutive years.

An avid skier with a commercial pop voice, Erec also rollerbladed for most of his years in New York City, shopping on Madison Avenue in his blades and skating regularly in five lanes of heavy traffic.

As a lifelong entrepreneur, this unbridled adventurer bases his decisions big and small on the whisper of his Inner Voice, which never led him to a typical 9-to-5 job.

With varying degrees of skill in shooting trap (ego-based decision), sailing (heart-pulled decision), calf-roping (thinking-mind decision), fly-fishing (wanting-to-look-cool decision), and water skiing (peer-pressure decision), Erec remains a true explorer who invites you to join him in online adventures as well.

Visit his website at www.ereclindberg.com and follow him on Facebook at https://www.facebook.com/erec.lindberg.

Your Inner Voice reminds you
that you are already what you seek to be.
Just trust the Inner Whisper and act on it.

Erec Lindberg

Congratulations! You finished reading the book!

Now you can add to what you have learned by working directly with Erec Lindberg.

Inner Voice Life Coaching

Erec works one-on-one with his clients as he helps them hear, trust, and act on their deepest Inner Voice callings. It is very powerful to work directly with Erec as you step into living the life you know you were always meant to live.

Contact Erec to schedule your complimentary discovery call and learn if his style is a fit for your next step. Go to www.ErecLindberg.com to schedule your session.

Inner Voice Mastermind

Erec offers Mastermind webinars that will take you deeper into developing a consistent practice of working with your Inner Voice directed insights. Increase your self-awareness of the daily nudges and pulls from within while gaining skills in hearing, trusting, and acting on your Inner Voice. This interactive learning will also help connect you with other like-minded people who are also striving to live their best lives.

See www.ErecLindberg.com for the latest details.

Inner Voice Keynote Speaker

Erec helps your audience members become aware that their Inner Voice is the most valuable asset they possess. He brings home the point that most of us were never taught at home or in school the skills needed to act on our Inner Voice for daily decisions. His stories will keep your audience on the edge of their seat. They will be enthralled with his combined skill of hearing, trusting, and acting on his Inner Voice in living his life. Your group members will be highly entertained and more connected to themselves with inspiration to listen to their own Inner Voice nudges.

Email Erec at ereclindberg@yahoo.com to discuss your event.

Inner Voice Podcast or Radio Guest

Erec is a fun, spontaneous, and very engaging live guest. He enthralls listeners with his witty personal stories of how his Inner Voice directed his unique successes. Erec explains the importance to take action with the energetic nudges of your Inner Voice. He teaches the three elements in how to gain skill with your Inner Voice.

Contact Erec at ereclindberg@yahoo.com to discuss your program.

Erec Lindberg and his dog Razzle Dazzle (Razz)

Printed in Great Britain
by Amazon